T0233271

Lecture Notes
in Business Information Processing   **217**

Series Editors

Wil van der Aalst
 Eindhoven Technical University, Eindhoven, The Netherlands
John Mylopoulos
 University of Trento, Povo, Italy
Michael Rosemann
 Queensland University of Technology, Brisbane, QLD, Australia
Michael J. Shaw
 University of Illinois, Urbana-Champaign, IL, USA
Clemens Szyperski
 Microsoft Research, Redmond, WA, USA

More information about this series at http://www.springer.com/series/7911

Artur Lugmayr (Ed.)

Enterprise Applications and Services in the Finance Industry

7th International Workshop, FinanceCom 2014
Sydney, Australia, December 2014
Revised Papers

 Springer

Editor
Artur Lugmayr
Curtin University
Perth, WA
Australia

ISSN 1865-1348   ISSN 1865-1356   (electronic)
Lecture Notes in Business Information Processing
ISBN 978-3-319-28150-6   ISBN 978-3-319-28151-3   (eBook)
DOI 10.1007/978-3-319-28151-3

Library of Congress Control Number: 2015958322

© Springer International Publishing Switzerland 2015
This work is subject to copyright. All rights are reserved by the Publisher, whether the whole or part of the material is concerned, specifically the rights of translation, reprinting, reuse of illustrations, recitation, broadcasting, reproduction on microfilms or in any other physical way, and transmission or information storage and retrieval, electronic adaptation, computer software, or by similar or dissimilar methodology now known or hereafter developed.
The use of general descriptive names, registered names, trademarks, service marks, etc. in this publication does not imply, even in the absence of a specific statement, that such names are exempt from the relevant protective laws and regulations and therefore free for general use.
The publisher, the authors and the editors are safe to assume that the advice and information in this book are believed to be true and accurate at the date of publication. Neither the publisher nor the authors or the editors give a warranty, express or implied, with respect to the material contained herein or for any errors or omissions that may have been made.

Printed on acid-free paper

This Springer imprint is published by SpringerNature
The registered company is Springer International Publishing AG Switzerland

Preface

Advancements in information and communication technologies have paved the way to new business models, markets, networks, services, and players in the financial services industry. To research these advancements, and invite international experts in the domain, we organized the FinanceCom Workshop in 2014 in Sydney to help us understand, drive, and exploit the associate systems, technologies, and opportunities. We invited experts from multiple disciplines, including technical, services, economic, sociological, media technology, and behavioral science to discuss the topic. We welcomed research work from any discipline, as the intention was to organize a cross-disciplinary workshop to leverage the knowledge of various fields. We were also open to any type of research analysis and methodology to explore this exciting topic.

FinanceCom is part of an extremely successful workshop series that has taken place in Regensburg (2005), Montreal (2007), Paris (2008), Frankfurt (2010), and Barcelona (2012). Most proceedings have been published as part of Springer's *Lecture Notes in Business Information Processing* series. The FinanceCom Workshop in 2014 in Sydney devoted its theme to "New Emergent Trends of IT in Finance Industry," and in particular sought themes in the following research areas:

- Networks and business models

  - Technology-driven transformation of the financial industry — towards banking value networks
  - Business process outsourcing/offshoring and information systems
  - New e-finance business models enabled by IT
  - New bank business models and challenges in a post-financial crisis
  - Approaches for evaluating operational and credit risks as well as banking and market performance

- Financial markets

  - Electronic markets design and engineering
  - Algorithmic and high-frequency trading/post-trading systems and infrastructures
  - Analysis of intraday market data and news
  - Regulation of electronic financial markets (e.g. MiFiD, EMIR or Dodd-Frank)
  - Private equity and Venture capital investments

- IT and implementations

  - Role of new technologies (e.g., Web services, cloud, big data, and grid computing)
  - Implementation experiences and case studies
  - Enabling decision support systems in banking and financial markets
  - Enterprise communication in banking and financial services

- Interoperability of heterogeneous financial systems and evolving international standards

- "New" emerging digital and virtual financial markets

  - Virtual Currencies (Bitcoin, Amazon, etc.)
  - Alternative banking, loan, and financial market models
  - New customer contact trends
  - Crowdfunding, crowdsourcing, and B2B/B2C social media
  - Loyalty card, and smart card markets
  - New consumer identification methods (e.g., biometrics)
  - M/T/I banking and trading services
  - New banking and payment trends

The workshop attracted over 35 international attendees; eight research papers and one invited paper were accepted for presentation at the workshop. The contribution from Maurice Peat and Stewart Jones from the University of Sydney, Australia, constituted an invited paper and presentation. There were also six industry presentations. Several works that have been contributed to these proceedings underwent a double-blind peer-review process.

The following section gives an overview of the accepted contributions. Accepted contributions related to various aspects of research in financial markets, and can be grouped into four major clusters: processing and evaluating market news, algorithms and pre-processing of data, enterprise systems and big data, and emerging trends in financial markets. In the following section, a brief overview of the particular contributions can be found, starting with the invited contribution from Maurice Peat and Stewart Jones from the University of Sydney, Australia:

- Invited Paper

  - "Detecting Changing Financial Relationships: A Self-Organizing Map Approach"; Maurice Peat (University of Sydney, Australia) et al. investigate Kohonen's self-organizing maps (SOMs) in the context of takeover target identification.

- Processing and Evaluating Market News

  - "Evaluation of News-Based Trading Strategies"; Stefan Feuerriegel (University of Freiburg, Germany) et al. investigate strategies for news-based trading with an emphasis on enabling decision support for financial markets, and demonstrate the sensitivity of financial markets to the release of news.
  - "A Framework for Evaluating the Effectiveness of Financial News Sentiment Scoring Techniques"; Islam Qudah (University of New South Wales, Australia) et al. investigate the efficiency of sentiment scores of financial news, compare potential models, and present a software architecture to cope with this challenge.
  - "Finding Evidence of Irrational Exuberance in the Oil Market"; Antal Ratku (University of Freiburg, Germany) et al. focus in particular on oil markets. They investigate the relation between the release of textual news disclosures, news reception, and market returns using the rolling window regression method.

- Algorithms and Data Pre-processing

  - "Validating an Incremental Rule Management Approach for Financial Market Data Pre-processing"; Weisi Chen (University of New South Wales, Australia) et al. devote their research work to data pre-processing, in particular in data quality aspects and data reliability aspects. The authors present a software tool that outperforms other tools in the domain.

- Enterprise Systems and Big Data

  - "Strategic Competitive Advantages Through Enterprise Systems: The Case of Exchange Systems"; Martin Haferkorn (Goethe University Frankfurt, Germany) et al. present how the upgrading of the IT infrastructure of exchange systems leads to competitive advantage and increases in trading volume.
  - "Conciliating Exploration and Exploitation at Middle-Manager Level: The Case Study of a European Bank Introducing Big Data"; Alberto Palazzesi (Università Cattolica del Sacro Cuore, Italy) et al. explore the exploitation of big data at an enterprise level based on research conducted within the context of the biggest European banks. The relationship between IT service provider, bank internal R&D departments, and middle management is investigated.

- Emerging Trends in Financial Markets

  - "Seasonality and Interconnectivity Within Cryptocurrencies – An Analysis of the Basis of Bitcoin, Litecoin, and Namecoin"; Martin Haferkorn (Goethe University Frankfurt, Germany) et al. describe how the market changes through the introduction of new technologies. With the example of cryptocurrencies, the authors illustrate how payment patters and behavior diverge with the introduction of cryptocurrencies.
  - "Survey of Financial Market Visualization Utilizing Interactive Media Technology"; Artur Lugmayr (Curtin University, Australia) presents a brief introduction to the use of the latest visualization technologies in financial industries.

In particular we would like to thank the Organizing Committee of the workshop, namely, Martin Aichner, Erste Group, Austria; Peter Gomber, University of Frankfurt, Germany; Dennis Kundisch, University of Paderborn, Germany; Artur Lugmayr, Tampere University of Technology, Finland; Nikolay Mehandjiev, University of Manchester, UK; Jan Muntermann, University of Goettingen, Germany; Dirk Neumann, University of Freiburg, Germany; Maurice Peat, University of Sydney, Australia; Fethi Rabhi, University of New South Wales, Australia; Ryan Riordan, University of Ontario, Canada; Christof Weinhardt, Karlsruhe Institute of Technology, Germany; Axel Winkelmann, University of Wuerzburg, Germany.

However, without our two sponsors, the University of Sydney, Australia, and SIRCA, Australia, the workshop would not have been possible. We would truly like to thank both sponsors!

If you are interested in joining the rather small community around financial markets, please feel free to join our mailing list, or browse through the workshop website. To post to the email list, please use the following email address: financecom@ ambientmediaassociation.org; if you would like to subscribe to the email list, please visit the following website: http://mail.ambientmediaassociation.org/mailman/listinfo/financecom_ambientmediaassociation.org

The workshop website, including programs and other arrangements, can be found at: www.ambientmediaassociation.org/tiki/article7-Workshop-Enterprise-Applications-Markets-and-Services-in-the-Finance-Industry-FinanceCom2014

Last but not least, by reading these proceedings, I wish you interesting insights into the latest research in financial markets.

October 2015   Artur Lugmayr

Contents

Detecting Changing Financial Relationships:
A Self Organising Map Approach

Maurice Peat[(⊠)] and Stewart Jones

The University of Sydney Business School,
University of Sydney, Sydney, NSW 2006, Australia
{maurice.peat,stewart.jones}@sydney.edu.au

Abstract. In this paper Kohonen's Self Organising Map is used as a tool for detecting changing financial relationships. A Self Organising Map (SOM) is a dimension reducing transform that maps an high dimension information set to a two dimensional grid that is amenable to visualisation. This dimension reduction step is a key component of all financial analysis tasks. The potential of this method to identify structural change is investigated in the context of the problem of takeover target identification. Use of SOM analysis on two samples from different time periods charts temporal instability in the information sets of sufficient magnitude to breach the stationarity assumptions of standard statistical modelling methods, the results are confirmed by probabilistic regression analysis. This finding helps to explain the poor discriminatory power of many takeover target prediction exercises.

Keywords: Self organising map · Financial stability · Takeover

1 Introduction

Recent events in financial markets have highlighted the instability of existing economic and financial relationships. One of the consequences of the breakdown in existing relationships is an associated reduction in the ability to use these relationships as the basis for prediction. Most predictive relationships extrapolate an existing relationship assuming that it will remain unchanged over the forecast window. A breakdown in predictability is a major problem for policy makers and market participants who engage in decision making based on predicted outcomes. Decision makers need to know when the relationships that underlie the predictions they are using have broken down. In the case of predictions based on time series models there is a well-documented approach to stationarity testing in one or more series, unit root and co-integration analysis. However, many relationships of interest to policy makers and analysts are not based on time series models. Activities that involve the assignment of economic entities to classes will generally not be based on time series models. They will typically be based on one of a number of methods that use characteristics of the entity to assign a class label to the entity.

At an abstract level financial analysis can be viewed as a two stage process; firstly mapping a high dimensional information set into a lower dimensional set, then partitioning the lower dimensional set on the basis of some attribute of the companies being

© Springer International Publishing Switzerland 2015
A. Lugmayr (Ed.): FinanceCom 2014, LNBIP 217, pp. 1–12, 2015.
DOI: 10.1007/978-3-319-28151-3_1

studied. Once the low dimensional set has been partitioned any company can be classified by passing its information through the mapping function to obtain its position relative to the partition in the lower dimensional set. The assignment of credit ratings is an example; a credit analyst assigns ratings (class labels) to entities based on a set of attributes of the entity and the state of the economic environment. Both the analysts and consumer of the ratings need to know if the relationships underlying the classification rules that generate the rating have changed through time. The bankruptcy prediction literature is another well known formal application of this two stage approach. In Altman [1] five financial ratios and an indicator of solvency are used as the information set for each company. The mapping from this five dimensional space to a one dimensional space is accomplished via a linear equation derived by applying the Linear Discriminate Analysis statistical technique. The partition of the resulting one dimensional set is based on the selection of a cut off value which minimises the number of misclassifications of solvency in the set of firms used in the estimation of the discriminate function.

The less formal judgemental approach used by analysts in the production of buy / sell recommendations also fits this approach. Financial information for the company of interest and a number of comparable companies is collected. Summary financial measures derived from the full information of the company and its peers are then used by the analyst to generate recommendations. The selection of the summary financial measures is analogous to the dimension reduction step and the analyst's decision rules leading to a recommendation are equivalent to the partitioning step.

The stability of the relationship between firm specific characteristics and the event of becoming a takeover target will be the subject of analysis. If it is possible to predict takeovers with accuracy greater than chance, it is possible to generate abnormal returns from holding a portfolio of the predicted targets, an objective that has proved difficult to achieve[1]. In the words of Barnes [2], "...*if the stock market is a casino, then anyone who can predict takeover targets will surely break the bank.*" Ideally there will be a stable functional relationship between a set of explanatory variables and becoming a takeover target. When the explanatory variables found to be significant explanitors are consistent with a well reasoned economic explanation of takeover activity, it is also reasonable to assume that they will remain significant over time. Inter-temporal consistency in the structure of firms information sets, stationarity, is a necessary condition for meaningful predictive accuracy.

A number of explanations of the drivers of takeover activity have been proposed. Jensen and Meckling [3] posit that agency problems occur when decision making and risk bearing are separated between management and stakeholders[2], leading to management inefficiencies. Manne [4] and Fama [5] theorised that a mechanism existed which ensured that management acted in the interests of the vast number of small

---

[1] Harris et al. (1982) found a predictive model with high explanatory power, which was unable to accurately discriminate between target and non target firms. Palepu (1986) provided evidence that the predictive ability of the logit model he constructed was no better than a chance selection of target and non target firms.

[2] Stakeholders are generally considered to be both stock and bond holders of a corporation.

non-controlling shareholders[3]. They suggest that a market for corporate control exists in which alternative management teams compete for the rights to control corporate assets. The threat of acquisition aligns management objectives with those of stakeholders as managers will be terminated in the event of an acquisition to rectify inefficient management of the firm's assets. Jensen and Ruback [6], suggest that both capital gains and increased dividends are available to an acquirer who can eliminate the inefficiencies created by target management, with the attractiveness of the firm for takeover increasing with the level of inefficiency.

Jensen [7] looks at the agency costs of free cash flow, another from of management inefficiency. In this case, free cash flow refers to cash flows in excess of positive NPV investment opportunities and normal levels of financial slack. The agency cost of free cash flow is the negative NPV value that arises from investing in these negative NPV projects rather than returning funds to investors. Jensen [7] suggests that the market value of the firm is discounted by the expected agency costs of free cash flow, he argues that these costs can be eliminated either by issuing debt to fund an acquisition of stock, or through merger or acquisition with/of a growing firm which has positive NPV investments that require the use of these excess funds. Smith and Kim [8] combine the financial pecking order argument of Myers and Majluf [9] with the free cash flow argument of Jensen [7] to create an another motivational hypothesis. Myers and Majluf [9] indicate that slack poor firms forgo profitable investment opportunities because of informational asymmetries. Jensen [7] argues that firms will undertake negative NPV projects rather than returning funds to investors. Smith and Kim [8] suggest that a combination of these firms, the slack poor and the slack rich firm, will be an optimal solution to the two respective resource allocation problems resulting in a market value for the combined entity which exceeds the sum of the individual values of the firms. This is one form of financial synergy that can arise in merger situations.

Jensen [7] also suggests that an optimal capital structure exists, where the marginal benefits and marginal costs of debt are equal. At this point, the cost of capital for a firm is minimised, which suggests that increases in leverage will only be viable for those firm's which suffer from free cash flow excesses, and not for those which have an already high level of debt. Lewellen [10] proposes that in certain situations, financial efficiencies may be realised even if no operational efficiencies are realised. Relying on a simple Miller and Modigliani [11] model, this proposes that increases in a firm's leverage to reasonable levels, in the absence of corporate taxes, will increase the value of the equity share of the company through realisation of a lower cost of capital. Lewellen [10] argues that a merger of two firms, where either of the firm's has not utilised its borrowing capacity, will result in a financial gain to the acquiring firm. This financial gain will represent a valuation gain above that of the sum of the equity values of the individual firms, but requires that the firms are unable to achieve this result without merger or acquisition. This is another form of financial synergy, which results from a combination of characteristics of the target and biding firms.

These theories provide a theoretical base for the selection of variables to explain takeover activity. They lead us to propose a number of hypotheses, which lead to nine

---

[3] We take the interests of shareholders to be in the maximization of the present value of the firm.

explanatory variables used as inputs to the SOM's constructed in each of the two time periods analysed.

2   Self Organising Maps

SOMs are a form of neural network which attempt to cluster data using an unsupervised learning algorithm proposed by Kohonen [12]. In an unsupervised learning environment it is not necessary to associate an output with an input data vector. The SOM projects the input data vectors into a low-dimensional space. Typically, the projection is onto a two-dimensional grid structure, allowing a visual representation of the high-dimensional input data.

Technically, a SOM is a neural network consisting of two layers; an input layer and the mapping layer (see Fig. 1). The input layer has as many nodes as there are input variables. The two layers are fully connected and each of the nodes in the hidden layer has an associated weight vector, with one weight for each connection with the input layer.

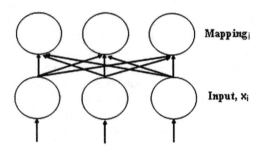

Fig. 1. Simple structure of a SOM.

The aim of a SOM is to group like input data vectors together on the mapping layer, the method is constructed to be topology preserving, so items which are close in the input space are close in the mapping space. During training data vectors are presented to the SOM through the input layer one at a time. The mapping node whose vector of incoming connection weights most closely resembles the components of the input data vector is assigned the input vector. This node has the values of its weight vector adjusted to move them towards the values of the input data vector, and the mapping layer nodes in the neighbourhood of the assigned node have their weight vectors updated to reflect the input data vector. As more input data is passed through the network, the weights of the mapping layer nodes will self-organise. By the end of the training process, regions on the mapping layer will represent regions in the higher dimensional input space. When the network has been trained, clusters in the output layer can be used to gain an understanding of the relationships in the underlying data.

The general training algorithm for the SOM is as follows:

- Initialise the weights between the input nodes and the mapping nodes to random values on the unit interval.
- Present an input vector x: $x_0, x_1, ..., x_{n-1}$.
- Calculate the Euclidian distance between the input vector and the weight vector for each mapping layer node j

$$d_j = \sum_{i=1}^{n-1} (x_i - w_{ij})^2 \tag{1}$$

- Select the mapping node j^* that has the minimum value of d_j.
- Update the weight vector for mapping node j^* and its neighbouring mapping nodes as follows:

$$w(t+1)_{ij} = w(t)_{ij} + \eta h(t)(x_i - w_{ij}) \tag{2}$$

where η is the learning rate of the map, and h defines a neighbourhood function. The neighbourhood size and the learning rate decline during training, in order to fine tune the developing SOM.
- Repeat steps (2)-(5) until the change in weights is less than a convergence criterion value.

In summary, SOMs are equivalent to a non linear, non-parametric regression that produces a topological, low-dimensional representation of data, which allows visualization of patterns and clustering in the data.

3   Method

3.1   Definition of Variables for Takeover Identification

The most commonly accepted motivational for takeovers is the *inefficient management hypothesis*; also known as the disciplinary motivation for takeovers. The suggestion of the hypothesis is that inefficiently managed firms will be acquired by more efficiently managed firms. The following variables are suggested by this hypothesis:

1. ROA (EBIT/Total Assets – Outside Equity Interests)
2. ROE (NPAT/Shareholders Equity – Outside Equity Interests)

A number of different effects of undervaluation on acquisition likelihood have been proposed. The competing explanations suggest a consistent impact of undervaluation on acquisition likelihood. The following variable is suggested by this explanation:

3. Market to book ratio (Market Value of Securities/Net Assets)

The *growth resource mismatch hypothesis* is the fourth hypothesis. Note, however, that the variables used to examine this hypothesis separately capture growth and resource availability. The following variables are suggested by this explanation:

4. Capital Expenditure/Total Assets
5. Current Ratio (Current Assets/Current Liabilities)

The *dividend payout hypothesis* suggests that firms which payout less of their earnings are doing so to maintain enough financial slack to exploit future growth opportunities as they arise. The following variable is suggested by this hypothesis:

6. Dividend Payout Ratio

Rectification of capital structure problems is an obvious motivation for takeovers, although there has been some argument as to the impact of low or high leverage on acquisition likelihood. This paper proposes a hypothesis known as the *inefficient financial structure hypothesis*. The following variables are suggested by this hypothesis:

7. Net Gearing (Short Term Debt + Long Term Debt)/Shareholders Equity
8. Long Term Debt/Total Assets

Size will have an impact on acquisition likelihood; it seems plausible that smaller firms will have a greater likelihood of acquisition, as larger firms generally will have fewer bidding firms with the resources to acquire them. The following variables are suggested by this explanation:

9. Ln (Total Assets)

It is standard practice in the development of neural networks and SOM's to normalise the input data to be distributed with zero mean and standard deviation of one.

3.2   Data

The data required to operationalise the variables defined is derived from the financial statements for Australian listed companies and balance sheet date price information. The financial statement information was sourced from the Aspect Huntley data base, which includes annual financial statement data for all ASX listed companies between 1995 and 2005. Lists of takeover bids and their respective success were obtained from the Connect4 database. This information makes possible the calculation of variables for relative merger activity between industries. Also, stock prices for the relevant reporting dates of all companies were sourced from the AspectHuntley online database, the Sirca Core Research Data Set, and Yahoo! Finance.

3.3   Sampling Schema

The sampling procedure was constructed to mimic the problem faced by a practitioner attempting to predict takeover targets into the future. The first sample that is used to establish the baseline relationship is based on financial data for the 2001 and 2002 financial years for firms that became takeover targets target between Jan 2003 to Dec 2004. The lag in the dates allows for the release of financial information and also allows for the release of financial statements for firms whose balance dates fall after the

30th June. A second sample is used to assess the stability of the model, this sample includes the financial data for the 2003 and 2004 financial years, which is used in conjunction with target and non target firms for the period Jan 2005 to Dec 2006. This sampling methodology allows for an evaluation of the functional stability of the relationship between financial characteristics and becoming a takeover target.

In the estimation of the maps and confirmatory modelling, we use a technique known as *state based sampling*. All target firms along with an equal number of randomly selected non target firms for the same period are used in the estimation of each map. Allison [13] suggests that using state based sampling, in cases where the dependent variable states are unequally distributed in the population, minimises the standard error of estimated parameters. Targets for the estimation sample are paired with a random sample of non target firms for the sample period, where financial data is measured over an identical period. This approach differs from matched pair samples where targets are matched to non targets on the basis of variables such as industry and/or size.

4   Results

Self Organising Maps are constructed for the data sets used in this study. A map is constructed for 2003 and 2005 takeovers, using a z normalisation over the whole data set for each variable. The maps constructed consist of 49 nodes arranged in a 7 by 7 grid. The maps are trained using the Kohonen library in R. The node weights are initialised to small random values. In the training of the map the observations are randomised and presented to the algorithm 500 times. A trained map consists of the variable weights for each node of the output layer and a distance minimising node assignment for each data vector used in the training of the map. A visual representation of each of these outputs can be constructed and used as tool to explore the stability of the structure represented by the data.

The map presented in Fig. 2 is known as a feature map. It is constructed from the node assignments of the training data. A score matrix for the map grid is constructed by adding one to the cell which corresponds to the node in the map that the observation is assigned to when the observation which is a target and subtracting one when the observation is not a target, the score matrix for the 2003 sample is presented in Table 1. The score matrix is in effect the result of a simple voting mechanism for the nodes, a node that has more targets than non targets mapped to it will have a positive tally, nodes with more non targets than targets will have a negative tally. The feature map is a grid graph of the score matrix using a gray scale to represent the tallies, the node with the highest number of associated targets is plotted in white and the node with the largest number of non targets is plotted in black.

The grid graph in Fig. 2 uses eleven shades of gray, the range of the tally values, to visualise the score matrix. Note that the graph plots the (1,1) cell of the score matrix in the bottom left corner, columns in the matrix are transposed to rows in the graph. The lighter the element in the grid the greater the number of target companies associated with the node represented by that element.

Table 1. Score matrix for 2003 takeovers using z normalized data.

	[,1]	[,2]	[,3]	[,4]	[,5]	[,6]	[,7]
[1,]	1	0	2	3	-1	4	2
[2,]	-1	0	2	2	-1	2	6
[3,]	-4	-2	-1	0	1	3	1
[4,]	0	1	-2	-1	-5	0	-1
[5,]	-2	0	-1	0	-3	1	2
[6,]	2	0	0	2	-2	-4	0
[7,]	-3	0	0	-2	0	0	-1

While Fig. 2 presents all of the information on the strength of association of each node in the map based on simple voting, it is difficult to delimit clusters of activity at this level of detail. The information in Fig. 2 can be simplified by defining a cluster matrix that corresponds to the score matrix. Each cell in the cluster matrix has a value of -1, 0 or 1; -1 for cells with more non takeovers, zero of ties and 1 for cells with more takeovers. When this matrix is plotted as a grid graph, which known as a cluster map, groupings of target and non-target companies are easily identified. The cluster map for takeovers in 2003 is presented in Fig. 3. Grid elements that are white represent votes won by target firms; elements in black represent votes won by non target firms and grey elements represent ties.

In terms of an analysis task involving a categorical recommendation, the ideal cluster map would contain a clean partition of the graph elements into a distinct region

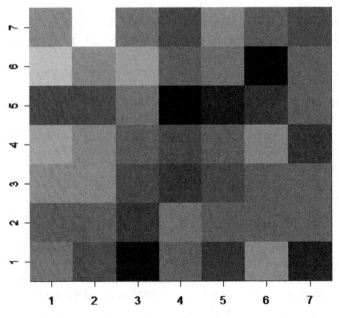

Fig. 2. Feature map of 2003 takeovers – z normalisation of variables.

for each class. In the case of takeover target identification the ideal map would contain only white and black elements, grouped into separable regions. The cluster map in Fig. 3 is not in this ideal form. There are two main clusters of target firms in the top left corner of the map, and four other isolated target elements which account for 34 % of the map elements. The non take over and tied elements account for the remaining 66 % of map elements. The fragmented nature of the target elements in the map indicate that a reliable rule for class assignment will be hard to discover using the current information set, a result that is born out in the lack of predictive accuracy reported in the takeover prediction literature.

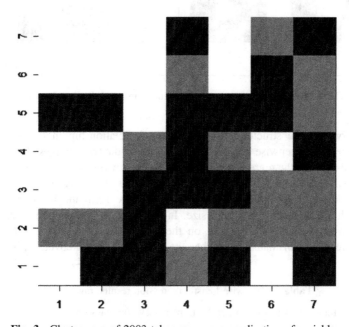

Fig. 3. Cluster map of 2003 takeovers – z normalisation of variables.

Stationarity of the relationships in the input data is a necessary condition for the development of a classification model which can be generalised. Testing for stationarity is well understood in the time series econometrics context. Testing for the stationarity of the joint distributions that underlie higher dimensional data sets, in a small sample context, is a less well understood problem. Analysts can use a comparison of a sequence of cluster maps to make a qualitative assessment of the stationarity of set of relationships within a data set. If the relationships are stable the structure of the cluster map will be retained over a sequence of maps at different points in time. A substantial change in the structure of the map is an indicator of a change in the relationships within the data set. Figure 4 shows the cluster maps for the z normalised data for 2005 on the left and 2003 on the right. The plots show a substantial change, the 2005 map displays a much higher degree of fragmentation in the target nodes, it also has fewer tied elements, with 90 % of the elements mapping to a specific state.

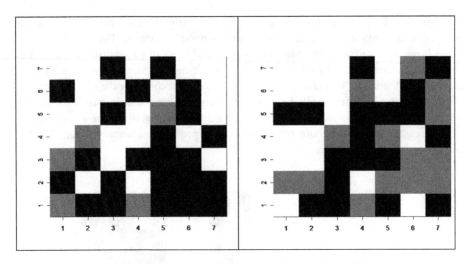

Fig. 4. Temporal stability of Z normalised cluster maps, 2005 and 2003 takeovers.

To verify that the structure of the underlying relationship in the data set has changed over time a stepwise logistic model is fitted to the two samples. Table 2 shows the results of running the regression procedure on the raw observations. The first model uses financial data from 2001 and 2002 to explain the takeovers observed in 2003. There are three significant explanatory variables, one from the resource mismatch group, the dividend payout ratio and size. In the case of the resource mismatch and dividend payout variables the impact on the probability of takeover is logical, the greater the resource mismatch the higher the probability of takeover, while dividend

Table 2. Stepwise logistic regression results, raw data.

Model 1 – Takeovers in 2003, Explanatory Variables observed in 2001-2002

	Value	Std. Error	t value
(Intercept)	-0.35256	0.21997	-1.60275
Capital Expenditure/Total Assets	0.318199	0.169599	1.876187
Dividend Payout Ratio	-0.27371	0.109557	-2.49834
Size	10.60865	2.280621	4.651649

Model 2 – Takeovers in 2005, Explanatory Variables observed in 2003-2004

	Value Std.	Error	t value
(Intercept)	-0.23539	0.157082	-1.49852
ROA	0.060563	0.032047	1.889797
Market to Book	0.139444	0.078859	1.768261
Size	4.422974	1.418297	3.11851

payments reduce the probability of takeover. The effect of size is counter intuitive; a large firm should be harder to takeover suggesting that the impact of size on takeover probability will be negative. The size result from this sample indicates that there were a number of large companies taken over in this period.

The second model estimates the probability of takeover in 2005 based on variables observed in 2003-2004. The stepwise procedure finds ROA, the Market to Book ratio and size to be significant explanatory variables. Of these variables only size is also a significant explanator in the model fitted in the earlier period. While the number of explanatory variables remains unchanged, variables related to inefficient management and undervaluation have replaced resource mismatch and the dividend payout ratio as explanatory variables in the model. These results show that the model based on the raw data is time sensitive, confirming the findings from the self-organising map analysis.

5 Conclusion

Recent turmoil in world finance has demonstrated the fragility of financial structures. The application of self organising maps to the problem of establishing the stability of financial relationships was explored in the context of a classification problem. In this study the temporal instability of the relationship between financial variables and firms taken over was demonstrated by applying self-organising maps and confirmed using a logistic regression analysis. The instability of this relationship helps to explain the observed inability to predict in this context. The self-organising map method can be used to explore the stability of the relationships that underlie any classification system. While the method does not provide a statistic in the classical sense, the graphical depiction, through cluster maps, of the evolution of the relationship provides the analyst with a clear view of changes in the underlying relationship.

Where there is a stable functional relationship between a set of explanatory variables and the probability of becoming takeover target meaningful predictive models can be constructed. The results presented suggest two areas of research which will help to advance target prediction modelling; the investigation of the process of model evolution using quarterly and half yearly financial reports and the introduction of dynamic elements, such as first difference variables into the modelling framework.

References

1. Altman, E.I.: Financial ratios, corporate bankruptcy. J. Finan. **23**, 589–609 (1968)
2. Barnes, P.: Predicting UK takeover targets: some methodological issues and empirical study. Rev. Quant. Finan. Account. **12**, 283–301 (1999)
3. Jensen, M.C., Meckling, W.H.: Theory of the Firm: Managerial behaviour, agency costs, and ownership structure. J. Finan. Econ. **3**, 305–360 (1976)
4. Manne, H.G.: Mergers and the market for corporate control. J. Polit. Econ. **73**, 110–120 (1965)
5. Fama, E.F.: Agency problems and the theory of the firm. J. Polit. Econ. **88**, 288–307 (1980)

6. Jensen, M.C., Ruback, R.S.: The market for corporate control: the scientific evidence. J. Finan. Econ. **11**, 5–50 (1983)
7. Jensen, M.C.: Agency costs of free cash flow. Corp. Finan. Takeovers, Am. Econ. Rev. **76**, 323–329 (1986)
8. Smith, R.L., Kim, J.-H.: The combined effect of free cash flow and financial slack on bidder and target stock returns. J. Bus. **67**, 281–310 (1994)
9. Myers, S.C., Majluf, N.S.: Corporate financing and investment decisions when firms have information that investors do not. J. Finan. Econ. **13**, 187–221 (1984)
10. Lewellen, W.G.: A pure financial rationale for the conglomerate merger. J. Finan. **26**, 521–537 (1971)
11. Miller, M.H., Modigliani, F.: Dividend policy. Growth, Valuation Shares, J. Bus. **34**, 411–433 (1964)
12. Kohonen, T.: Self-organized formation of topologically correct feature maps. Biol. Cybern. **43**, 59–69 (1982)
13. Allison, P.D.: Logistic Regression Using the SAS System. SAS Institute, Cary, NC (2006)

Evaluation of News-Based Trading Strategies

Stefan Feuerriegel[(✉)] and Dirk Neumann

Information Systems Research, University of Freiburg, Platz der Alten Synagoge,
79098 Freiburg, Germany
`stefan.feuerriegel@is.uni-freiburg.de`

Abstract. The marvel of markets lies in the fact that dispersed information is instantaneously processed by adjusting the price of goods, services and assets. Financial markets are particularly efficient when it comes to processing information; such information is typically embedded in textual news that is then interpreted by investors. Quite recently, researchers have started to automatically determine news sentiment in order to explain stock price movements. Interestingly, this so-called news sentiment works fairly well in explaining stock returns. In this paper, we attempt to design trading strategies that are built on textual news in order to obtain higher profits than benchmark strategies achieve. Essentially, we succeed by showing evidence that a news-based trading strategy indeed outperforms our benchmarks by a 9.06-fold performance.

Keywords: Financial news · Decision support · Trading strategies · Text mining · Sentiment analysis

1 Introduction

Market efficiency relies, to a large extent, upon the availability of information. Nowadays, market information can be accessed easily as it comes naïvely with the prevalence of electronic markets and, because of the straightforward access, decision makers can use such information (e.g. [18]) to make purchases and sales more beneficial. In the same context, the so-called (weak) efficient market hypothesis [11] asserts that financial markets are *informationally efficient*, in the sense that financial stock prices accurately reflect all public information at all times; price adjustments occur when previously unknown information enters the market, as is the case with *news*.

Several publications (e.g. [5,6,43]) study the market reception of news announcements, finding a causal and clearly measurable relationship between financial disclosures and stock market reaction. Market reception is not only triggered by the quantitative facts embedded in financial disclosures, but, more importantly, qualitative information drives stock market reactions to financial disclosures, since news is typically embodied in text messages. In order to extract tone from a textual content, one frequently measures the polarity of news by measuring the so-called *news sentiment*.

© Springer International Publishing Switzerland 2015
A. Lugmayr (Ed.): FinanceCom 2014, LNBIP 217, pp. 13–28, 2015.
DOI: 10.1007/978-3-319-28151-3_2

While previous research [2, 21, 47, 48] succeeded in establishing a link between news tone and stock market prices, it is not clear how the extracted sentiment signals can then be utilized to facilitate investment decisions. To close this gap, this paper studies how news sentiment, as an emergent trend of IT in the finance industry, can enrich news-based trading. News trading combines real-time market data and natural language processing to detect suitable news announcements in order to trigger transactions. Its mechanisms are often part of an algorithmic trading system, while many regard it as an enabling Decision Support System (DSS) for use in banking and financial markets [16].

Consequently, this paper investigates how a Decision Support System can utilize news sentiment to perform stock trading in practice. Overall, our contribution is as follows: first, we propose different rule-based trading strategies. Second, we find quantitative evidence that our news trading system can outperform benchmark scenarios. In addition, news-based trading profits from incorporating other external variables, such as price momentum, to achieve better estimates of possible market reaction in that specific economic cycle.

The remainder of this paper is structured as follows. In Sect. 2, we review related research on the sentiment analysis of financial disclosures and news trading, in which we focus particularly on how both can be tied within a trading system. Next, Sect. 3 describes the data sources, as well as the news corpus, that is integrated into the sentiment analysis to extract the subjective tone of financial disclosures. The calculated sentiment values are then integrated (Sect. 4) into various news trading strategies and, finally, Sect. 5 evaluates these strategies in terms of their financial performance.

2   Related Work

In this section, we present related literature grouped into two categories: first, we compare algorithmic approaches that measure news sentiment in financial disclosures. Second, we review previous works from both IT and finance that distill news into trading actions as part of a decision support system for investments.

2.1   News Sentiment in the Financial Domain

Methods that use the textual representation of documents to measure the positivity and negativity of the content are referred to as opinion mining or *sentiment analysis*. Sentiment analysis can be utilized to extract subjective information from text sources, as well as to measure how market participants perceive and react to financial materials. In this case, one uses the observed price reactions following financial text to validate the accuracy of the news sentiment. Based upon sentiment measures, one can study the relationship between financial documents and their effect on markets. Empirical evidence, for example, shows that a discernible relationship between news content and stock market reaction exists, see e. g. [2, 47] for some of the first analyses.

As sentiment analysis is applied to a broad variety of domains and textual sources, research has devised various approaches to measure sentiment. A recent literature overview [37] provides a comprehensive domain-independent survey and, within the domain of finance, a number of surveys [32,35] compare studies aimed at stock market prediction. For example, *dictionary-based approaches* are very frequently used in recent financial text mining research [8,21,23,29,48]. These methods count the frequency of pre-defined positive and negative words from a given dictionary, producing results that are straightforward and reliable. In comparison, *machine learning approaches* [2,28,34,41, for example] offer a broad range of methods, but may suffer from overfitting [42].

In this paper, we want to address only the trading simulation itself and so utilize a dictionary-based approach to allow for easier verification of our results. Furthermore, dictionary approaches seem to be the more widespread technique nowadays in finance literature.

2.2   News Trading

This section provides a brief overview of components that are necessary for a news trading system. A more detailed review and taxonomy can be found in [16]. In behavioral finance, news trading has long been associated with both noise and arbitrage trading [3]. Noise traders chase profit from overreactions to momentary events, whereas arbitrageurs exploit mispricing, possibly indicated by news stories [44,45]. As a consequence, both a lack of information and misunderstanding may contribute to gains [1,31] from news trading. Most likely, an even larger advantage would result from automated transactions that a Decision Support System could trigger, before human information processing triggered a buy/sell decision, following news releases.

As a first key ingredient for a realistic study of news trading, we need to account for incurred *transaction fees*. Several previous research papers perform trading simulations, but many neglect the importance of transaction fees.

- For example, a support vector machine using financial news yields an accuracy of 71 % in predicting the direction of asset returns [41]. Overall, this gives an excess return of 2.88 % compared to the S&P 500 index between October 25, 2005 and November 28, 2005. A different approach uses decision rules with risk words [27] which yields an average annual excess of 20 % compared to U. S. Treasury bills. Similarly, Tetlock [47] incorporates pessimistic words and yields a 7.3 % plus, when compared to the Dow Jones, with the applied trading strategy. However, all the aforementioned papers share a lack of consideration for transaction fees, which, in fact, can be substantial [20].
- One of the few papers that considers transaction fees also utilizes German ad hoc announcements and yields an accuracy of 65 % when predicting the direction of returns. Along with transaction fees of 0.1 %, the average return per transaction accounts for 1.1 %. However, this paper [20] relies on one basic strategy (similar to our simple news-based strategy) and does not compare other trading strategies.

As a second addition to our Decision Support System, we need to test our trading strategies using *benchmark scenarios*. A common approach is to utilize a benchmark stock index for comparison. The author of [49] predicts the direction of stock price movements via sparse matrix factorization utilizing news articles from the Wall Street Journal. The results show an accuracy rate of 55.7 %, higher than when compared to a reference index. As an alternative, related research also integrates simple buy-and-hold strategies of stocks with the highest historic returns.

The third component of a news trading system involves *trading strategies*. Simple buy-and-hold strategies are common when testing news trading in historic portfolio simulation. For example, the authors of [25] hypothesize that a sentiment-based selection strategy outperforms a classical buy-and-hold benchmark strategy (holding all stocks over the whole test period). This approach is what the authors call a portfolio selection test. In a different paper [33], the authors build a news categorization and trading system to predict stock price trends. The system is combined with a trading engine that generates trading recommendations in the form of *"buy stock X and hold it until the stock prices hit the +d % barrier"*. In a similar fashion, a trading strategy can be built around the Google query volume [39] for search terms related to finance. This variable is integrated into a simple buy-and-hold strategy (without transaction costs) to buy the Dow Jones index at the beginning and sell it at the end of the hold period, in which the authors tested various lengths of holding strategies. This strategy yields a 16 % profit, equal to the overall increase in value of the Dow Jones index in the time period from January 2004 until February 2011.

3   Background

This section introduces background knowledge for both datasets and the sentiment analysis. First, we describe the construction of the news corpus that is used throughout this paper. We then transform this running text into machine-readable tokens to measure news sentiment.

3.1   Data Sources

Our news corpus originates from regulated ad hoc announcements[1]. These announcements must be published for all listed firms in Germany in English. We choose this data source primarily because companies are bound to disclose these ad hoc announcements as soon as possible through standardized channels, thereby enabling us to study the short-term effect of news disclosures on stock prices. In research, ad hoc announcements are a frequent choice [35] when it comes to evaluating and comparing methods for sentiment analysis. In addition, this type of news corpus shows several advantages: ad hoc announcements must be authorized by company executives, the content is quality-checked by the

---

[1] Kindly provided by Deutsche Gesellschaft für Ad-Hoc-Publizität (DGAP).

Federal Financial Supervisory Authority[2] and several publications analyze their relevance to the stock market – finding a direct relationship (e. g. [14,15,36]).

Our collected announcements date from the beginning of January 2004 until the end of June 2011. We investigate such a long time period to avoid the possibility of only analyzing news driven predominantly by a single market event, for example, the financial crisis. In addition, we apply the following *filter rules*. First, each announcement must have at least 50 words. Second, we focus only on ad hoc press releases from German companies which are written in the English language. Our final corpus consists of 14,463 ad hoc announcements. To study stock market reaction, we use the daily stock market returns of the corresponding company, originating from Thomson Reuters Datastream. We only include business days and, due to data availability, we yield a total of 2108 observations. In addition, we adjust the publication days of ad hoc announcements according to the opening times of the stock exchange. This is achieved by counting all disclosures after 8 p.m. to the next day.

We later also integrate a stock market index into our analysis as follows: in our analysis, the so-called CDAX index works as a benchmark which the trading strategies need to combat in terms of performance. The CDAX (see Fig. 1) is a German stock market index calculated by Deutsche Börse. It is a composite index of all stocks traded on the Frankfurt Stock Exchange that are listed in the General Standard or Prime Standard market segments, giving a total of 485 stocks. It does not contain foreign firms or foreign stocks, thus serving as a suitable match to our ad hoc news corpus.

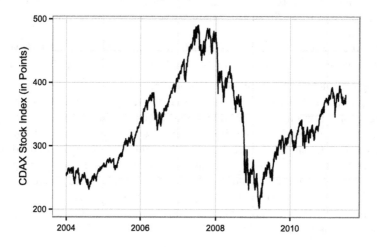

Fig. 1. The CDAX as a German stock market index representing our benchmark.

---

[2] Bundesanstalt für Finanzdienstleistungsaufsicht (BaFin).

3.2   Sentiment Analysis

Methods that use the textual representation of documents to measure positive and negative content are referred to as opinion mining or *sentiment analysis* [37]. In fact, sentiment analysis can be utilized [32,35] to extract subjective information from text sources, as well as to measure how market participants perceive and react to news. One uses the observed stock price reactions following a news announcement to validate the accuracy of the sentiment analysis routines. Thus, sentiment analysis provides an effective tool chain to study the relationship between news content and its market reception [2,12,47].

Before performing the actual sentiment analysis, there are several preprocessing steps as follows:

1. **Tokenization.** Corpus entries are split into single words named *tokens* [19].
2. **Negations.** Negations invert the meaning of words and sentences [7,40]. When encountering the word *no*, each of the subsequent three words (i.e the object) are counted as words from the opposite dictionary. When other negating terms are encountered (*rather, hardly, couldn't, wasn't, didn't, wouldn't, shouldn't, weren't, don't, doesn't, haven't, hasn't, won't, hadn't, never*), the meaning of all succeeding words is inverted.
3. **Stop Word Removal.** Words without a deeper meaning, such as *the, is, of,* etc. are named *stop words* [30] and can be removed. We use a list of 571 stop words proposed in [26].
4. **Synonym Merging.** Synonyms, though spelled differently, convey the same meaning. In order to group synonyms by their meaning, we follow a method that is referred to as pseudoword generation [30]. Approximately 150 frequent synonyms or phrases from the finance domain are aggregated according to their meanings.
5. **Stemming.** Stemming refers to the process of reducing inflected words to their stem [30]. Here, we use the so-called Porter stemming algorithm [38].

Having completed the preprocessing, we can continue to analyze news sentiment. As shown in a recent study [13] on the robustness of sentiment analysis, the correlation between news sentiment and stock market returns varies across different sentiment metrics. A sentiment approach that results in a reliable correlation is the Net-Optimism metric [8]. Net-Optimism works well in coordination with Henry's Finance-Specific Dictionary [21]. Consequently, we rely upon this approach in the following evaluation. The metric is calculated as the difference between the number of positive $W_{\mathrm{pos}}(A)$ and negative $W_{\mathrm{neg}}(A)$ words divided by the total number of words $W_{\mathrm{tot}}(A)$ in an announcement A. Thus, Net-Optimism sentiment $S(A)$ is defined by

$$S(A) = \frac{W_{\mathrm{pos}}(A) - W_{\mathrm{neg}}(A)}{W_{\mathrm{tot}}(A)} \in [-1, +1].\qquad(1)$$

4   Trading Strategies

This section introduces all the trading strategies that serve as a foundation for our analysis. Consistent with the existing literature, we start by presenting our benchmark, namely, a momentum trading approach. This strategy derives purchase decisions solely from the historic returns of assets by maximizing the so-called rate-of-change. In addition, we propose news-based trading strategies in which investment decisions are triggered by news sentiment signals. Then, we combine both methods and develop a strategy that utilizes both historic prices and news sentiment.

In the subsequent algorithms, we use the following notation: let $p_{i,t}$ denote the closing price of a stock i at time t. Furthermore, the variable $S(A)$ gives the news sentiment of an announcement A corresponding to stock i as defined above.

When trading, we exclude all so-called penny stocks (i.e stocks below €5) from our evaluation [4,9]. The reason behind this is that these penny stocks tend to react more unsystematically to trends and news announcements and, consequently, may introduce a larger noise component to our data.

4.1   Benchmark: Momentum Trading

Past stock returns can be a predictor of future firm performance. This is what we define as *momentum*, in which historic stock prices continue moving in their previous direction. The (partly) predictable connection between past and future return has been proven in the finance literature, such as in [22]. Nevertheless, finance academics have trouble with the finding that a simple strategy of buying winners and selling losers can apparently be profitable, since this contradicts the theory of efficient markets [11], where markets quickly absorb new information and adjust asset prices accordingly. Momentum is, consequently, also named a *"premier anomaly"* in stock returns [10]. By extrapolating historic stock trends, we motivate the following *momentum trading*, which picks up the subtle patterns in returns. Developing a successful momentum trading strategy is primarily a merit from the manual efforts of finance academics and practitioners to hand-engineer features from historical prices [46].

Let us define both the terms momentum and rate-of-change respectively. The so-called *momentum $Mom_{i,t}$* is the absolute difference in stock i defined by

$$Mom_{i,t} = p_{i,t} - p_{i,t-\delta} \tag{2}$$

with a time span of δ days. In short, momentum denotes the difference between today's closing price and the closing price N days ago, thus referring to prices continuing to trend. In comparison, the *rate-of-change RoC_i* represents the relative change as a fraction, i.e

$$RoC_{i,t} = \frac{p_{i,t} - p_{i,t-\delta}}{p_{i,t-\delta}} = \frac{Mom_{i,t}}{p_{i,t-\delta}}. \tag{3}$$

Both the momentum and rate-of-change indicators indicate trend by remaining positive during an uptrend or negative during a downtrend.

Altogether, this results in the momentum trading strategy [24], formally introduced by the following pseudocode. In short, the key idea is to always choose the stock that has the highest rate-of-change. Step 1 initializes the variable s which stores the stock that our Decision Support System currently holds. The subsequent for-loop iterates through all time steps of our simulation horizon T. In each iteration, Step 3 updates the rate-of-change scales for all stocks, excluding the current business day. If the previously held stock was empty, then Step 5 invests in the stock with the highest absolute value of all historic rate-of-change values. However, if the rate-of-change of the currently held stock drops below a threshold θ_{RoC}, then we trigger transactions to sell the previous stock (Step 7) and buy (or short-sell) new stock with the highest rate-of-change in Step 8.

As free parameters, we can vary the time span δ calculating the rate-of-change and the threshold θ_{RoC}. For the former, we find good results with δ set to 200 business days. This value serves as a good trade-off in between the range of 20 days to 12 months proposed in the literature [22]. We choose the latter variable θ_{RoC} by testing different values, and decide for $\theta_{\mathrm{RoC}} = 50\,\%$.

1: Initialize stock $s \leftarrow \perp$.
2: **for** t **in** T **do**
3:     Compute $RoC_{i,t-1} \leftarrow \dfrac{p_{i,t-1} - p_{i,t-1-\delta}}{p_{i,t-1-\delta}}$ for all stocks i.
4:     **if** $s = \perp$ **then**
5:         Buy or short-sell stock $s \leftarrow \arg\max_{i} |RoC_i|$.
6:     **else if** $|RoC_{s,t-1}| < \theta_{\mathrm{RoC}}$ **then**
7:         Remove investment in stock s.
8:         Buy or short-sell stock $s \leftarrow \arg\max_{i} |RoC_i|$.
9:     **end if**
10: **end for**

4.2 News Trading

While the previous strategy only utilizes historic stock prices, we now instead focus on news sentiment in order to enable news-based purchase decisions. In order to react to news sentiment signals, our Decision Support System needs to continuously scan the news stream and compute the sentiment once a new financial disclosure is released. When the news sentiment associated with this press release is either extremely positive or negative, this implies a strong likelihood of a subsequent stock market reaction in the same direction. We benefit from the stock market reaction if an automated transaction is triggered beforehand.

To achieve this goal, we specify the so-called simple *news trading strategy*, given in the pseudocode below. Steps 2 and 3 trigger buy and short-sell decisions, whenever the absolute value of the news sentiment metric of an incoming announcement exceeds a certain positive or negative threshold. This decision is given by the if-statement in Step 1, i.e the condition that $S(A)$ is smaller than a negative threshold θ_S^- or larger than a positive θ_S^+ must be fulfilled. We choose suitable threshold values for both θ_S^- and θ_S^+ as part of our evaluation in Sect. 5.

Input: Released announcement A that corresponds to stock i.

1: **if** $S(A) > \theta_S^+$ **or** $S(A) < \theta_S^-$ **then**
2:    Remove investment in previous stock s.
3:    Buy or short-sell stock $s \leftarrow i$.
4: **end if**

4.3   Combined Strategy with News and Momentum Trading

The subsequent trading strategy combines the above approaches by utilizing both news sentiment and historic prices in the form of momentum. We develop this trading strategy around the idea that we want to invest in assets with both (1) a news disclosure with a high polarity and (2) a previous momentum in the same direction. The combined pseudocode is given below. Only if both the news release and historic prices give an indication of a development in the same direction, Steps 3 and 4 trigger a corresponding trading decision. Thus, this strategy expects the same direction in terms of the return-of-change and sentiment metric as tested in Step 2.

Input: Released announcement A that corresponds to stock i at day t.

1: Compute $RoC_{i,t-1} \leftarrow \dfrac{p_{i,t-1} - p_{i,t-1-\delta}}{p_{i,t-1-\delta}}$ for stock i.
2: **if** $|S(A)| > \theta_S$ **and** $\mathrm{sign}\, S(A) = \mathrm{sign}\, RoC_{i,t-1}$ **then**
3:    Remove investment in stock s.
4:    Buy or short-sell stock $s \leftarrow i$.
5: **end if**

5   Evaluation

The above sections have presented a number of trading strategies that differ in the way in which operations are derived; this section evaluates these trading strategies in terms of their achieved performance. We first focus on our benchmark strategies, i.e momentum trading and German composite stock market index. We then determine suitable values for all free parameters inside the news trading algorithms and analyze their performance.

5.1   Benchmarks: Stock Market Index and Momentum Trading

As our first benchmark, we choose the so-called CDAX, a German stock market index calculated by Deutsche Börse. It is a composite index of all stocks traded on the Frankfurt Stock Exchange that are listed in the General Standard or Prime Standard market segments. Figure 1 shows the overall development of the stock index from the year 2004 until mid-2011. During that period, the index increased by 50.99 %, which correspond to 5.65 % at an annualized rate. The number of days with positive returns outweigh the negative days by 1092 to 864.

Simple momentum trading acts as our second benchmark. This strategy works with no data input other than historic stock prices. When historic prices continue their trend, we can invest in the specific stock to profit from this development. While news trading yields high returns at first, the profits later plummet, resulting in a negative cumulative return of -65.33%. Nevertheless, the average daily returns remain positive at 0.0464% and are even higher than that of the CDAX index (0.0298%). The number of days with positive returns outweighs the negative by 1154 to 767.

The results of both benchmarks, namely, the CDAX stock market index and momentum trading, are presented in Fig. 2 where we see different performance patterns.

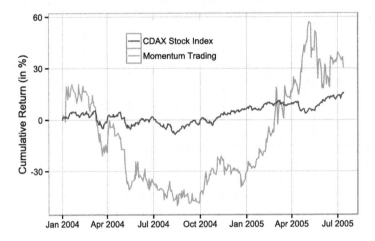

Fig. 2. Cumulative returns of both the CDAX index and the momentum trading strategy compared across the first 400 business days.

5.2 News Trading

This section evaluates different variants of news trading, starting with a simple trading strategy. This strategy triggers transactions whenever a very positive or negative ad hoc announcement is disclosed. Here, we take into account only a single announcement per day and business days, giving a total corpus of 1894 disclosures.

What remains unanswered thus far is av value for the threshold θ_S above which our news-based trading strategies perform a purchase decision. In order to find the optimal parameter, Fig. 3 compares the thresholds θ_S^+ and θ_S^- against the average returns. For reasons of simplicity, we measure these thresholds in terms of quantiles of the news sentiment distribution. We see that a threshold value of around 10 % appears in a cluster of high daily returns and yields good results. Thus, we decided to set θ_S^+ to the 90 % quantile (and θ_S^- to the 10 % quantile) of the sentiment values $S(A)$ in order to make this variable exogenously given. However, it is important to stress that there large variations in performance depending on the threshold.

Evaluating the above strategies with historic data reveals the following findings:

- With the threshold set to the 10 % quantile, we gain an overall cumulative return of 178.53 % at a volatility of 0.078. The average daily return accounts for 0.421 %.
- In addition, we include a combination of news and momentum trading. This strategy leads to a lower performance with a cumulative return of 361.60 % and average daily returns of 0.1180 %. However, this strategy simultaneously reveals a reduced risk component in the form of less volatility, which accounts for 0.028.

Both strategies, namely, simple news trading and the combined version, are further evaluated in the following diagrams. Figure 4 depicts how the cumulative returns develop during the first 1500 business days, showing clearly the superiority of simple news trading.

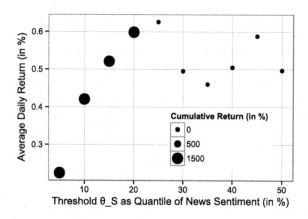

Fig. 3. Comparison of thresholds θ_S^+ and θ_S^- against average daily returns. The threshold is measured as quantiles from both ends of the average news sentiment in the corpus. In addition, the point size indicates the total cumulative return.

5.3 Comparison

The simulation horizon spans January 2014 until the end of June 2011, giving a total of 1956 business days. All results of our trading simulation are provided

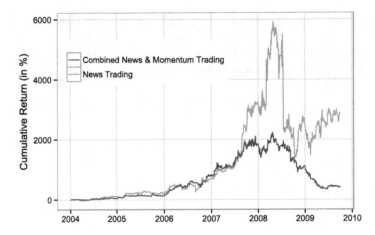

Fig. 4. Cumulative returns of both news trading and the combination of news and momentum trading compared across the first 1500 business days.

in Table 1. Here, we evaluate how well the investment decisions of each strategy play together with market feedback. We focus mainly on average daily return, since cumulative returns can be misleading. The reason is as follows: one wrong trade can make performance plummet, while a high average daily return indicates a continuously high benefit. In addition, we want to direct attention to the volatility column. These values serve as an indicator of the level of risk associated with each strategy. Even though simple news trading achieves higher returns, it is linked with higher volatility and higher risks. Thus, it may be beneficial for practitioners to follow a combined strategy of news and momentum trading that results in smaller returns, while also decreasing the associated risk.

We now compare our benchmarks to news trading. The benchmarks feature mean returns of 0.0298 % for the CDAX and 0.0464 % for momentum trading. In comparison, news trading reaches 0.4206 %. This is the 9.06-fold value, but linked with a considerably higher volatility.

While we put an emphasis on raw returns, we also provide a performance measure that incorporates transaction costs. Thus, the last column of Table 1 reveals how an initial invest of €1000 would evolve over time. Consistent with [20, 48][3], we simulate the portfolio with a transaction fee for each buy/sell operation of 0.1 %, equivalent to 10 bps.[4]

---

[3] Using a proportional transaction fee is common in financial research. For example, other papers [17] mostly vary transaction costs mostly in the range of 0.1 % to 0.3 % or assume a fixed transaction fee [33] of U. S. $ 10 for buying and selling stocks respectively.

[4] A frequent unit in finance is basis point (bps). Here, one unit is equal to 1/100th of 1 %, i.e 1 % = 100 bps.

Table 1. Comparison of benchmarks and trading strategies across several key performance characteristics.

Trading strategy	Cumulative return	Returns: median	Returns: mean	Annualized return	#Positive returns	#Negative returns	Volatility	ΔTrades	Portfolio outcome (€)
Benchmarks									
CDAX Index	50.99 %	0.0703 %	0.0298 %	5.6480 %	1092	864	0.01319	—	1506.92
Momentum Trading ($\theta = 50\%$, $\delta = 200d$)	−65.33 %	0.0000 %	0.0464 %	−13.1702 %	1129	827	0.04496	102.95d	322.94
News Trading									
Simple News Trading ($\theta_S^+ = 90\%$, $\theta_S^- = 10\%$)	17853.31 %	0.0000 %	0.4206 %	99.7803 %	1136	820	0.07780	10.57d	967448.60
Combined: News &Momentum ($\theta_S^+ = 90\%$, $\theta_S^- = 10\%$, $\delta = 200d$)	361.60 %	0.0000 %	0.1180 %	22.6222 %	1113	843	0.02839	19.96d	9513.92

6   Conclusion and Outlook

Although it is a well-known fact that financial markets are very sensitive to the release of financial disclosures, the way in which this information is received is far from being studied sufficiently. Not until recently have researchers started to look at the content of news stories using very simple techniques to determine news sentiment. Typically, these research papers concentrate on finding a link between the qualitative content and the subsequent stock market reaction. To harness this relationship in practice, news trading combines real-time market data and sentiment analysis in order to trigger investment decisions. Interestingly, what previous approaches all have in common is that they rarely study and compare trading strategies.

As a remedy, this paper evaluates algorithmic trading strategies within a Decision Support System for news trading. We propose and compare different rule-based strategies for news-based trading. As a result, our Decision Support System outperforms all benchmark scenarios by relying upon news-based investment decisions. Further performance improvements can be achieved by including external variables that, for example, describe the economic environment or lagged prices respectively. Altogether, we contribute to the understanding of information processing in electronic markets and show how to enable decision support in financial markets.

This paper opens avenues for further research into two directions. First, a multi-asset strategy could be beneficial to spread risks. To model these, intriguing approaches include Value-at-Risk (VaR) measures, as well as techniques from portfolio optimization. Second, it is worthwhile to improve the forecast of asset returns by including a broader set of exogenous predictors. As such, possible external variables range from stock market indices, fundamentals describing the economy and additional lagged variables. Further enhancements would also result from embedding innovative news sources, such as social media. Altogether, the accuracy of predicting stock return directions and trigger trading signals would be greatly improved.

References

1. Alfano, S.J., Feuerriegel, S., Neumann, D.: Is news sentiment more than just noise? In: 23rd European Conference on Information Systems (ECIS 2015), Münster, Germany, 26-29 May 2015
2. Antweiler, W., Frank, M.Z.: Is all that talk just noise? The information content of internet stock message boards. J. Finance **59**(3), 1259–1294 (2004)
3. Barberis, N., Thaler, R.: A Survey of Behavioral Finance. Financial Markets and Asset Pricing. Handbook of the Economics of Finance, pp. 1053–1128. Elsevier, Amsterdam (2003)
4. Beatty, R., Kadiyala, P.: Impact of the penny stock reform act of 1990 on the Initial public offering market. J. Law Econ. **46**(2), 517–541 (2003)
5. Cenesizoglu,T.: The reaction of stock returns to news about fundamentals. Management Science (2014)
6. Cutler, D.M., Poterba, J.M., Summers, L.H.: What moves stock prices? J. Portfolio Manag. **15**(3), 4–12 (1989)

7. Dadvar, M., Hauff, C., de Jong, F.: Scope of negation detection in sentiment analysis. In: Proceedings of the Dutch-Belgian Information Retrieval Workshop (DIR 2011), Amsterdam and Netherlands, pp. 16–20 (2011)
8. Demers, E.A., Vega, C.: Soft Information in Earnings Announcements: News or Noise? INSEAD Working Paper No. 2010/33/AC, SSRN Electronic Journal (2010)
9. Fama, E.F., French, K.R.: Multifactor explanations of asset pricing anomalies. J. Finance **51**(1), 55–84 (1996)
10. Fama, E.F., French, K.R.: Dissecting anomalies. J. Finance **63**(4), 1653–1678 (2008)
11. Fama, F.E.: The behavior of stock-market prices. J. Bus. **38**(1), 34–105 (1965)
12. Feuerriegel, S., Heitzmann, S.F., Neumann, D.: Do investors read too much into news? How news sentiment causes price formation. In: 48th Hawaii International Conference on System Sciences (HICSS) (2015)
13. Feuerriegel, S., Neumann, D.: News or noise? How news drives commodity prices. In: Proceedings of the International Conference on Information Systems (ICIS 2013), Association for Information Systems (2013)
14. Ratku, A., Feuerriegel, S., Rabhi, F., Neumann, D.: Finding evidence of irrational exuberance in the oil market. In: Workshop on Enterprise Applications, Markets and Services in the Finance Industry, FinanceCom 2014, Sydney, Australia, December 12, 2014, to be published in Springer's LNBIP (2014)
15. Feuerriegel, S., Ratku, A., Neumann, D.: Analysis of how underlying topics in financial news affect stock prices using latent dirichlet allocation. In: Proceedings of the 49th Hawaii International Conference on System Sciences (HICSS), Kauai, January 5–8, 2016, IEEE Computer Society (2016)
16. Gagnon, S.: Rules-based integration of news-trading algorithms. J. Trading **8**(1), 15–27 (2013)
17. Graf, F.: Mechanically Extracted Company Signals and their Impact on Stock and Credit Markets (2011)
18. Granados, N., Gupta, A., Kauffman, R.J.: Research commentary-information transparency in business-to-consumer markets: concepts, framework, and research agenda. Inf. Syst. Res. **21**(2), 207–226 (2010)
19. Grefenstette, G., Tapanainen, P.: What is a word, what is a sentence? Problems of Tokenization (1994)
20. Hagenau, M., Liebmann, M., Hedwig, M., Neumann, D.: Automated news reading: stock price prediction based on financial news using context-specific features. In: 45th Hawaii International Conference on System Sciences (HICSS), pp. 1040–1049 (2012)
21. Henry, E.: Are investors influenced by how earnings press releases are written? J. Bus. Commun. **45**(4), 363–407 (2008)
22. Jegadeesh, N., Titman, S.: Returns to buying winners and selling losers: implications for stock market efficiency. J. Finance **48**(1), 65–91 (1993)
23. Jegadeesh, N., Di, W.: Word power: a new approach for content analysis. J. Financ. Econ. **110**(3), 712–729 (2013)
24. Kim, K.: Financial time series forecasting using support vector machines. Neurocomputing **55**(1–2), 307–319 (2003)
25. Klein, A., Altuntas, O., Hausser, T., Kessler, W.: Extracting investor sentiment from weblog texts: a knowledge-based approach. In: IEEE 13th Conference on Commerce and Enterprise Computing (CEC), pp. 1–9 (2011)
26. Lewis, D.D., Yang, Y., Rose, T.G., Li, F.: RCV1: A new benchmark collection for text categorization research. J. Machine Learning Res. **5**, 361–397 (2004)

27. Li, F.: Do stock market investors understand the risk sentiment of corporate annual reports? SSRN Electronic Journal (2006)
28. Li, F.: The information content of forward-looking statements in corporate filings: a Naïve Bayesian Machine learning approach. J. Account. Res. **48**(5), 1049–1102 (2010)
29. Loughran, T., McDonald, B.: When is a liability not a liability? Textual analysis, dictionaries, and 10-Ks. J. Finance **66**(1), 35–65 (2011)
30. Manning, C.D., Schütze, H.: Foundations of Statistical Natural Language Processing. MIT Press, Cambridge (1999)
31. Mendel, B., Shleifer, A.: Chasing Noise. J. Financ. Econ. **104**(2), 303–320 (2012)
32. Minev, M., Schommer, C., Theoharry G.: News And Stock Markets: A Survey On Abnormal Returns and Prediction Models (2012)
33. Mittermayer, M.A.: Forecasting intraday stock price trends with text mining techniques. In: Sprague, R.H. (ed.) the 37th Annual Hawaii International Conference on System Sciences, (2004) IEEE Computer Society Proceedings of Los Alamitos, California
34. Mittermayer, M.A., Knolmayer, G.F.: NewsCATS: A news categorization and trading system. In: Sixth International Conference on Data Mining (ICDM'06), pp. 1002–1007 (2006)
35. Mittermayer, M.A., Knolmayer, G.F.: Text Mining Systems for Market Response to News: A Survey (2006)
36. Muntermann, J., Guettler, A.: Intraday stock price effects of ad hoc disclosures: the German case. J. Int. Finan. Markets. Institutions and Money **17**(1), 1–24 (2007)
37. Pang, B., Lee, L.: Opinion mining and sentiment analysis. FNT Inf. Retrieval **2**(1–2), 1–135 (2008)
38. Porter, M.F.: An algorithm for suffix stripping. Program **14**(3), 130–137 (1980)
39. Preis, T., Moat, H.S., Stanley, H.E.: Quantifying trading behavior in financial markets using Google Trends. Sci. Rep. **3**, 1684 (2013)
40. Pröllochs, N., Feuerriegel, S., Neumann, D.: Enhancing sentiment analysis of financial news by detecting negation scopes. In: 48th Hawaii International Conference on System Sciences (HICSS), pp. 959–968 (2015, Forthcoming)
41. Schumaker, R.P., Chen, H.: Textual analysis of stock market prediction using breaking financial news. ACM Trans. Inf. Syst. **27**(2), 1–19 (2009)
42. Sharma, A., Dey. S.: A comparative Study of Feature selection and machine learning techniques for sentiment analysis. In: Cho, Y. (ed.) and ACM Special Interest Group on Applied Computing: Proceedings of the 2012 Research in Applied Computation Symposium (RACS 2012), pp. 1–7 (2012). ACM, New York
43. Shiller, R.J.: Irrational Exuberance. Princeton University Press, Princeton (2005)
44. Shleifer, A., Summers, L.H.: The noise trader approach to finance. J. Econ. Perspect. **4**(2), 19–33 (1990)
45. Shleifer, A., Vishny, R.W.: The limits of arbitrage. J. Finance **52**(1), 35–55 (1997)
46. Takeuchi, L., Lee, Y.Y.: Applying Deep Learning to Enhance Momentum Trading Strategies in Stocks (2013)
47. Tetlock, P.C.: Giving content to investor sentiment: the role of media in the stock market. J. Finance **62**(3), 1139–1168 (2007)
48. Tetlock, P.C., Saar-Tsechansky, M., Macskassy, S.: More than words: quantifying language to measure firms' fundamentals. J. Finance **63**(3), 1437–1467 (2008)
49. Wong, F.M.F., Liu, Z., Chiang, M.: Stock market prediction from WSJ: text mining via sparse matrix factorization. In: IEEE International Conference on Data Mining (ICDM), pp. 430–439. IEEE Computer Society, Shenzhen, China (2014)

A Proposed Framework for Evaluating the Effectiveness of Financial News Sentiment Scoring Datasets

Islam Qudah[1](✉), Fethi A. Rabhi[1](✉), and Maurice Peat[2]

[1] School of Computer Science and Engineering,
University of New South Wales, Sydney 2052, Australia
{ialqudah, fethir}@cse.unsw.edu.au
[2] Business School, University of Sydney, Sydney 2006, Australia
maurice.peat@sydney.edu.au

Abstract. The impact of financial news on financial markets has been studied extensively. A number of news sentiment scoring techniques are being widely used in research and industry. However, results from sentiment studies are hard to interpret contextual and sentiment related parameters change. Sometimes, the conditions which lead to the results are not fully documented and the results are not repeatable. Based on service-oriented computing principles, this paper proposes a framework that automates the process of incorporating different contextual parameters when running news sentiment impact studies. The framework also preserves the set of parameters/dataset and conditions for the end user to enable them to reproduce their results. This is demonstrated using a case study that shows how end users can flexibly select different contextual and sentiment related parameters and conduct news impact studies on daily stock prices.

Keywords: Sentiment analysis · Financial news · Stock returns · News analytics · Event studies · ADAGE · TRNA

1 Introduction

As a result of the internet revolution, analyzing news and social media information has become increasingly important for the survival of many businesses. Consequently, sentiment analysis has flourished and become an important research area as it has applications in many domains, like media and marketing. This research is concerned with analyzing the impact of both scheduled news and unscheduled news in the financial domain. Robertson et al. [48] describe the complex interdependencies between different news sources and the different roles assumed by data sources such as news providers and aggregators. Figure 1 illustrates the different types of news with a focus on the finance area. We can see that news not only originate in traditional channels (newspapers, TV, Radio and Internet) but increasingly in social media (blogs, message boards, Facebook and Twitter). Companies listed on a stock exchange release news to the media as required by regulation and when they feel the need to, for instance to introduce a new product or to refute rumors about the company performance [35].

© Springer International Publishing Switzerland 2015
A. Lugmayr (Ed.): FinanceCom 2014, LNBIP 217, pp. 29–47, 2015.
DOI: 10.1007/978-3-319-28151-3_3

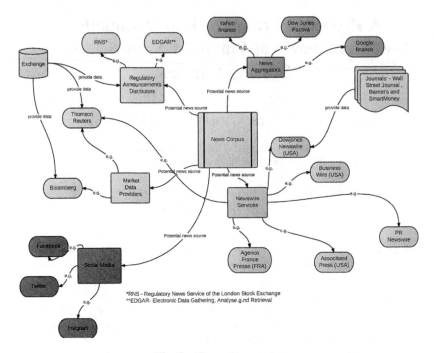

Fig. 1. News source types

The paper reviews the techniques currently used to conduct sentiment analysis of news in the financial domain and shows that there is huge variety in the contexts being addressed and the way the impact of a technique is measured. Its main contribution is to propose a framework for evaluating sentiment scoring techniques in a systematic way.

The paper is structured as follows. The next section gives some background on the different types of techniques used for sentiment analysis and presents various approaches for measuring the impact on financial markets with an overview of existing research studies in this space. Section 3 proposes a new framework for carrying out the evaluation of sentiment scoring techniques. Section 4 describes a prototype and some preliminary results. Finally, Sect. 5 concludes this paper.

2 Background

2.1 News Sentiment Analysis Lifecycle

Sentiment analysis literature depicts the analysis of news and extraction of sentiment information as a complex process, because it can be decomposed into sub-processes. We broadly consider these sub processes as acquiring news, extracting news and context characteristics and finally calculating sentiment metrics. This general process is illustrated in Fig. 2.

News acquisition involves accessing external sources and downloading news data. It includes some pre-processing tasks such as filtering to eliminate superfluous or

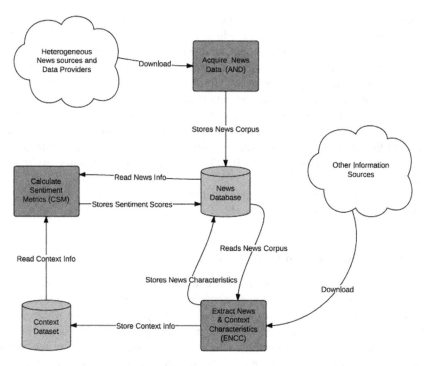

Fig. 2. News analytics processes

redundant information and the storing of news data in a database. At this stage, a typical news record will have a type, some attributes and free text. News types and attributes provided are dependent on the news source. For example, Thomson Reuters [58, 59] classifies its news into four different types {Alert, Headline, StoryAppend, StoryOverwrite} and provides attributes like company codes and topic codes with every news record.

Following news acquisition, there are a range of techniques which extract additional information from the news corpus or from external information sources. Some of these techniques enrich news records in the corpus with new information, some examples are:

- Text pre-processing: Reduce news corpus text by applying common pre-processing techniques found in the literature including; tokenization, removing stop words, and stemming [31, 37].
- Named entity recognition [8]: associating unique names to objects, for example names of companies, people and locations. There are many systems that produce named entities like Thomson Reuters OpenCalais [58], Stanford Named Entity Recognizer [54], GATE [61] and CMCRC/Fairfax's system [42].
- Categorisation: adding categories to news according to criteria such as: news topic, news novelty, news relevance etc. This information could be provided by the news provider, obtained from external sources or computed using text analysis software [2, 20, 46].

News analytics attributes may also be obtained through analysis of the news corpus in conjunction with other data sources, which could be passed to the next phase via a context database. Such information can include: Word weightings from techniques such as bag of words, feature extraction and representation techniques and Term Frequency–Inverse Document Frequency (TF-IDF), these techniques are discussed in detail in [38]. Word weighing techniques aim at discriminating between different words in terms of their weight factor/loading e.g. weigh a word "buy" as stronger than word like "position" [17, 33, 38]. Other news attributes are volume of news [46, 59], seasonality of the news [1, 2, 20, 28], search volume index [16, 62] for example Google search volume index, news bias ratio [10, 17] and others. These attributes are listed in Table 1 in Sect. 2.3 below.

The final phase is to calculate sentiment metrics for a given news story based on information produced by previous phases.

2.2   Overview of News Sentiment Analysis Techniques

The first issue related to conducting news sentiment analysis is to define what is being analysed i.e. is it all records in the database or only certain types of records (e.g. headlines). Within the chosen record type does the analysis concern the whole text or each sentence separately? Aspect level sentiment analysis focuses on analyzing the different attributes in a news record as some attributes could have positive scores and some negative scores. Understanding the sentiment around each attribute is necessary if we want to reach a higher level of sentiment accuracy [32].

The second issue is to decide on the metrics that should be used to represent news sentiment. The simplest representation of a sentiment in the literature is a {positive, negative} dichotomy, some researchers consider neutral as an additional class. A sentiment score is a numeric value which can be mapped into a sentiment class. The sentiment score expresses the strength of the sentiment, usually represented as a value between (-1 ∼ extremely negative) and (+1 ∼ extremely positive) with zero being neutral. Sentiment about an entity could be expressed in a comparative way, for example "Honda has better steering control than Nissan". Jindal and Liu [26] used supervised learning models to extract comparative sentences from news documents and customer reviews. They use comparative adjectives like: more, less, and words ending with 'er' like for example 'longer' or 'higher'. They mined superlative adjectives and adverbs like: most, least, and words ending with 'est' such as: coolest, finest. They achieved 81 % classification accuracy [26]. Another study focused on extracting sequential patterns from text. This technique uses a naïve Bayes classifier approach to filter out any sentence that does not have comparative syntax. Then using a Class sequential pattern mining algorithm, it parses the sentences looking for entities based on a pre-prepared set of seed entities. The algorithm stops when no more entities are discovered.

There are many algorithms proposed for sentiment classification that are based on detecting words (or named entities) in free text [3–5, 17, 45, 49, 56, 57]. They vary depending on how positive/negative words are identified and the way a news sentiment score is computed, aggregating the scores of constituent words or named entities. The process of feature extraction and aggregation can use unsupervised or supervised learning methods. Unsupervised learning is used in situations in which an external lexicon (dictionary), usually hand authored by humans, such as WordNet [43], or the Harvard IV-4 dictionary can be utilized to determine the sentiment orientation of a document [52, 55]. Loughran and McDonald in [33] authored a sentiment dictionary for the finance domain.

Supervised learning techniques include: Naïve Bayes Classifier, Support Vector Machines, Logistic Regression or KNN [27, 39]. The accuracy of supervised learning algorithms depend heavily on the accuracy of the feature selection technique applied [32]. The most popular feature selection and representation techniques are: bags of words, terms and their frequencies, terms presence, Term Frequency–Inverse Document Frequency (TF-IDF), Part of Speech(POS) and information and sentiment lexicons are explained in more detail in [32, 38]. Supervised learning models require a set of training inputs, labeled manually by humans. They are specific to a domain like finance, politics, movie reviews or product reviews and require extensive time and effort to achieve high classification accuracy. Azar found in [5] that a sentiment system trained to classify financial news performed poorly when running on movie review posts. Similar approaches used to classify documents can be used to classify sentences. Wiebe et al. in [63] used a naïve Bayes classifier to extract subjective sentences. Pang and Lee [40] used a minimum cut approach to classify subjective sentences, assuming that neighboring sentences usually carry the same sentiment as the sentence being analyzed. Other researchers [36] have argued that one single approach to classify sentences does not work with all types of sentences. Therefore, different approaches have to be used to classify conditional sentences, or sentences containing sarcasm. Narayanan et al. [36] analyzed subjectivity and sentiment polarity in conditional sentences, where 8 % of text written is of conditional nature. They used supervised learning models (SVM algorithm) to analyze news documents.

Instead of using bag of words approaches, sentiment analysis can focus on the whole text itself using Natural Language Processing (NLP) techniques. They work by extracting the semantic orientation of a set of phrases in a news document, determining the sentiment orientation for each phrase and then applying a weighting scheme to calculate the sentiment orientation for the whole document e.g. Turney [60]. Natural Language understanding (NLU) is a subtopic of NLP and is focused on understanding the semantics of news [13]. Concept based approaches [12] rely on semantic sentiment analysis rather than syntactic sentiment analysis of text. Semantic sentiment analysis is based on ontologies containing huge resources of affective concepts and their semantics e.g. SenticNet [51]. Other semantic ontologies supported by popular research bodies include Microsoft's Probose, Princeton's WordNet [43] and MIT's ConceptNet [14]. An evaluation by Cambria and his team at MIT of these three major semantic ontologies shows ConceptNet/SenticNet was the most accurate ontology system.

2.3   Determining the Impact of a News Sentiment Analysis Technique

Having described the processes used to calculate sentiment metrics, we now turn our attention to the way researchers determine how informative a sentiment analysis technique is, by measuring the impact of news on financial markets. We first present some basic assumptions e.g. what is being impacted by the news, then discuss ways to measure impact in a quantitative way.

There are a range of financial markets theories, such as the efficient market hypothesis with it is three forms, strong, semi-strong and weak. Some alternative approaches are: cognitive theories which discuss investor's motive to make buying/selling decisions and more recent adaptive theories, where the investor takes a trial/error approach to making buy/sell decisions [9, 24]. A number of market impact measures have been used to gauge the impact of news, stock returns are the most popular market measure [15, 23, 33, 36]. Trading volume and liquidity are alternative market measures used widely in the literature [17, 24]. Price to earnings ratio, cost of capital and risk level [24, 29, 34] are less frequently observed measures that have been used to assess impact.

That financial market impact measures are affected by the sentiment in news is evident in many studies [34]. There is an extensive literature around measuring the impact of certain types of news on financial markets in specific contexts. Tables 1 and 2 illustrate the news variables used to predict and explain various market impact measures. Table 1 describes the news analytics attributes found in the literature, and how these attributes were used to study impact.

Table 1. News analytics literature summary

Research Study/ Variables	News relevance	Optimism/ Pessimism Score	News Volume	News Novelty (Uniqueness)	News bias ratio	News type, Head line keyword	News topic	Investor Attention Volume	Sentiment scores
[56]		✓							
[29]									✓
[11]			✓						
[2]			✓	✓			✓		
[1]			✓		✓				
[20]	✓		✓	✓	✓				
[47]			✓						
[17]			✓		✓				
[18]							✓	✓	
[16]								✓	
[22]			✓						
[50]			✓						
[67]									✓
[52]								✓	✓
[4]			✓						✓
[7]			✓						
[21]									✓

News analytics and sentiment analysis surveys [68, 69] reviewed studies focusing on analyzing news to explain/predict financial markets. They highlighted the need for future studies to be more aware of context, given that correlating news and financial market measures can be performed in many contexts. For instance an entity could react to news differently when the context is changed. To date the relationship between different contexts and sentiment scores has not been placed in a formal framework.

Table 2. Impact measures literature summary

Research Study/ Variables	Cost of capital	Large Stocks	Market Reaction Speed	Market Opening hour/Operating Hours	Volatility	Stock Returns	Trade Volume	Investor Reaction speed	Risk Level	Insider Trading
[56]						✓				
[29]	✓				✓				✓	
[11]		✓	✓							
[2]		✓	✓	✓						
[1]			✓		✓	✓				
[20]			✓	✓		✓				
[47]			✓		✓					
[17]					✓	✓	✓			
[18]			✓			✓				
[16]						✓				
[22]								✓		
[50]								✓		
[67]									✓	
[52]						✓	✓			
[4]			✓		✓	✓	✓			
[7]						✓				
[21]										✓

3 Research Problem and Research Methodology

3.1 Research Gap and Research Methodology

Most of the results described in the literature concerning sentiment analysis are difficult to reproduce outside a specific context, i.e. there is a lack of transparency in conducting sentiment analysis studies. Existing studies perform data analysis using custom-built systems that lack the flexibility to allow the user to conduct many studies on the same set of data using different parameters or to compare different datasets using the same parameters. To reproduce a studies' results, one would need to implement the algorithms (sentiment techniques) and have access to the input (news & market) data used. This makes the task of reproducing results a complex job [25, 41]. Moreover the metrics used for comparison can change (stock returns, risk level …etc.). It is a challenge to automate the process of incorporating the contextual parameters required to run news impact studies.

Based on the research problem, we propose a model that allows contextual variables to be set when comparing sentiment scoring techniques. The system will also allow different impact measures to be used, the proposed comparison parameters model will be described in more details in Sect. 3.2. The model will be supported by software infrastructure that automates the process of data acquisition, analysis and results presentation (to be discussed in Sect. 3.3). Finally, a case study will be used to demonstrate the viability of this approach using an existing sentiment scoring dataset (see Sect. 4).

3.2   Proposed Comparison Parameters Model (CPM)

The proposed solution introduces a comparison parameters model that allows users to flexibly choose which parameters they are interested in evaluating. The model consists of context parameters, sentiment data parameters and impact measures.

Context Related Parameters (*C*). As a first step, the user needs to define the parameters that define a context around the question "What is the impact of news on an entity (E)?". Such parameters include:

- E: Identity of the entity being impacted by the news e.g. a company, an industry sector, the economy of a country as a whole.
- EV: A variable associated with the entity in question whose value is impacted e.g. closing share price, an index, GDP etc.
- B: A benchmark against which the impact will be measured
- BV: A value indicative of the selected benchmark
- P: The period during which the experiment takes place
- EP: The estimation period used to measure impact

All these context parameters are defined as a context vector, C. Where $C = (E, Ev, B, Bv, P, EP)$.

Sentiment Related Functions. The second step is defining sentiment functions relevant to the dataset being analysed. We assume the existence of a news sentiment dataset (X) containing a number of news records. Each record, X, has a list of attributes $\{a1, a2....an\}$ such as: sentiment class (negative, positive, neutral), sentiment score, news item topic, headline keywords, news relevance to an entity. The model defines the following functions:

- Filter Function $(Fn(a1...an, X))$: Fn filters dataset X by attributes which are determined by the user $\{a1...an\}$ and returns *True* or *False*.
- Extreme news selection function $T(X)$: a threshold function that defines "extreme" scores, used to select the news whose impact will be measured.

The results of applying both functions are stored in the subset, Y of X.

Impact Measure Parameter (*IM*). The model allows for the specification of how to measure the impact of news sentiment on the entity (E), relative to the benchmark (B). In this paper we will use the event study methodology to measure impact [24], because it is a widely used technique in the finance domain. Accordingly we will calculate the Mean Accumulative Abnormal Returns (MCAR) on a daily basis to measure impact [24]. A limitation of this measure is evident when more than one news story is released on a particular day, which makes it difficult to determine which news story had more impact on the entity (E). In addition, news stories could cancel each other's impact if they have opposing sentiment orientation (i.e. one extreme negative news and one extreme positive news could neutralise the impact (Ev) on entity (E) on the day they were both released.

3.3   Proposed Model Implementation

The proposed model needs to be supported by a software infrastructure that facilitates the reproducibility of experiments using different parameters. The following steps (see Fig. 3) illustrate how the proposed prototype works:

(a) Step 1 - Select Context parameters (C): User selects the context parameters ($C = \{E, Ev, B, Bv, EP, P\}$).
(b) Step 2– Select Impact Measure (*IM*): User Selects the Impact measure (IM).
(c) Step 3- Import Market Data for selected (C, IM); Market data imported is determined by the context parameters C and by the Impact Measure (*IM*) selected in first and second steps.
(d) Step 4- Select Sentiment parameters: User defines the sentiment related functions (Fn, T).
(e) Step 5- Process sentiment dataset (X): Sentiment functions (Fn, T) are used to process the sentiment dataset (X) and generate a subset of extreme news called (Y).
(f) Step 6- Perform Impact Analysis: Conduct event studies based on extreme events in sentiment dataset (Y) using impact measure (*IM*).

The case study described in the next section details an application of the proposed model and its implementation.

3.4   Proposed Prototype Implementation

To ensure reliability we have focused our implementation on an existing, well established framework called ADAGE described in [44], which stands for Ad-hoc DAta Grid Environment. For the purpose of the case study, we have customized the ADAGE framework as follows:

- A web service has been implemented to acquire and filter news analytics and sentiment datasets from the Thomson Reuters News Analytics datasets [70].
- We have reused existing ADAGE services to import daily stock prices from TRTH and for building time series.
- We have developed a service for performing event studies using Eventus [71].
- We used the TAVERNA open source workflow management system [72] to develop workflows for acquiring market data, building time series and conducting event studies.
- A Web-based GUI has been developed for specifying parameters, launching the workflows and visualizing abnormal return patterns

4   Case Study

To evaluate the validity of the proposed model, we devised a case study to demonstrate flexibility, reproducibility issues and more importantly, to understand how context and sentiment parameters are interrelated. The case study consists of a number of

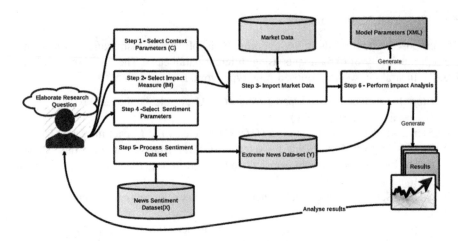

Fig. 3. Proposed prototype

experiments designed to demonstrate the efficacy of the proposed comparison parameters model (CPM). First we set the comparison parameters model values. Using the selected parameters, the proposed model is executed and the results are discussed.

4.1 Defining Parameters for the Case Study

The experiments were designed to study the effect of extreme negative news on a small number of Australian companies during 2011. As Table 3 shows, the context will be assessing the impact of news on the closing price of these companies, using the All Ordinaries market index as a benchmark. We are using Reuters Instrument Codes (RIC) to uniquely represent listed companies and indices.

The case study uses Thomson Reuters News Analytics (TRNA) dataset accessed via Sirca [53] as the target news sentiment dataset (X). The TRNA dataset offers the following news related attributes:

Table 3. Setting context parameters

Context variable (C)	Value	Description
Entity (E)	RIC = {BHP.AX,QAN.AX}	Listed Australian company
Entity Variable (Ev)	Closing price	Daily closing price of company
Benchmark (B)	RIC = .AORDA	All ordinaries market index which lists top

(Continued)

Table 3. (*Continued*)

Context variable (*C*)	Value	Description
		500 Australian listed companies [66] is used as a benchmark
Benchmark Variable (*Bv*)	Closing value	Daily closing value of index
Study Period (*P*)	(1/01/2011,31/12/2011)	The period during which the experiment takes place. For the purpose of this case study we assume one year worth of news data is considered large enough to work with
Estimation Period (*EP*)	200 days	Number of days used for estimation, before and after an event

- **Reuters Instrument Code (RIC):** an instrument unique identifier associated to the news item.
- **News Relevance (R):** an attribute which defines how relevant the news item is to the RIC. Values range from (0 non relevant) to (1 highly relevant).
- **News Topic (NT):** each news item is related to a certain topic/s, denoted as *NT*. Examples: AIR for air transport news, BKRT for bankruptcy related news.
- **News Item Story Release Date (SRD):** news story release date and time.
- **Sentiment Class (SC):** new items sentiment orientation. TRNA classifies news into three classes (Positive with score of 1, Negative with score -1 and Neutral with score 0).
- **Sentiment Score (SS):** each news item has sentiment score ranging from 0 neutral/no sentiment to 1 extreme sentiment score.

The experiments will use different filter functions based on the above attributes. Two threshold functions (*T*1 and *T*2) are utilised to identify extremely negative news. First we introduce the following notations:

$$\left\{ \begin{array}{l} n_{a=} \text{attribute } a \text{ of news record } n \\ \mu_a(S) = \text{The mean of } n_a \text{ in dataset } (S) \\ _a(S) = \text{The standard deviation of } n_a \text{ in dataset } (S) \end{array} \right.$$

$T1(X)$ and $T2(X)$ are defined as follows:

1. T1(X)=
    V= Select all news records where n_{sc}= -1
    $t = \mu_{ss}(V)+ {}_{ss}(V)$
    For every news record n in V do
        If n_{ss}> t then add record n to Subset Y end if

        End For
        Return (Y)

2. T2(X) =
    V= Select all news records where n_{sc}= -1
    t= $\mu_{ss}(V)$+ ½ $_{ss}(V)$
    For every day d in V do
        BP = Select all news records where n_{sc}= -1
        BN = Select all news records where n_{sc}= +1
        d = $\mu_{ss}(BN)$ - $\mu_{ss}(BP)$
        If $d > t$ then include subset (BN) in subset Y end if
    End For
    Return (Y)

T1 selects news stories with negative sentiment measures more than one standard deviation from the average. *T2* selects negative news stories when the difference in sentiment between positive and negative stories on the day is half a standard deviation from the average sentiment value.

4.2   Experiments

All experiments used TRNA data for 2011, the dataset contains 1120444 distinct news stories, where 667890 of the news entries are classified by TRNA as positive and 452554 are classified as negative. This dataset contains news about 24814 different companies listed on stock exchanges worldwide, averaging around 45 news items per company.

All experiments used the parameters in Table 4. The experiments are conducted on two large companies listed on the Australian Stock Exchange, BHP Billiton (BHP.AX) and Qantas (QAN.AX). During 2011 BHP.AX had a total of 2066 news records (1109 negative, 957 positive) and Qantas had 564 news records (391 negative, 173 positive).

4.3   Results

The 8 experiments conducted produced the results displayed in Table 5. The column (No. of Extreme Negative News|Y|) lists the total number of news stories per experiment. The column (No. of Distinct Event Days) contains the number of event days in dataset (Y). In addition, the table also lists the results for the end of day returns. The impact measure, *IM*, for this paper is (Mean Cumulative Abnormal Return (MCAR)) of

Table 4. Experiments parameters

Exp. No.	Context Parameters	Sentiment Parameters		Dataset size	
	Entity (E)	Fn (RIC, R, NT, SRD, SC, SS)	Tn	$|Fn(X)|$	$|Y|$
1	QAN.AX	RIC= QAN.AX, R=1, SRD={ 01/01/2011, 31/12/2011}	$T1$	203	83
2	QAN.AX	RIC= QAN.AX, R=1, SRD={ 01/01/2011, 31/12/2011}, NT= 'O'	$T1$	14	7
3	QAN.AX	RIC= QAN.AX, R=1, SRD={ 01/01/2011, 31/12/2011}, NT='JOB'	$T1$	56	20
4	BHP.AX	RIC= BHP.AX, R=1, SRD={ 01/01/2011, 31/12/2011}	$T1$	322	132
5	BHP.AX	RIC= BHP.AX, R=1, SRD={ 01/01/2011, 31/12/2011}, NT= 'O'	$T1$	31	7
6	BHP.AX	RIC= BHP.AX, R=1, SRD={ 01/01/2011, 31/12/2011}, NT='JOB'	$T1$	26	14
7	QAN.AX	RIC= QAN.AX, R=1, SRD={ 01/01/2011, 31/12/2011}	$T2$	203	19
8	BHP.AX	RIC= BHP.AX, R=1, SRD={ 01/01/2011, 31/12/2011}	$T2$	322	12

entity (E) in relative to benchmark (B). Lastly the column (Generalized Sign Z) highlights the statistical significance of the returns. The symbols \$, *, **, and *** denote statistical significance at the 0.10, 0.05, 0.01 and 0.001 levels, respectively, using a generic one-tail test for non-zero MCAR.

The following observations can be made by examining the MCAR column's figures in Table 5:

- Experiments 1 to 6 which implemented ($T1$) the one standard deviation threshold approach show that measuring the impact using MCAR is not meaningful, because negative news are associated with positive MCAR in 4 experiments (1, 2, 3, 5). The reason being on those days both negative and positive stories were released. For instance 6 news stories with high positive sentiment scores were released about BHP responding to the labor strikes news released on the same days. Similarly Qantas had 4 positive news stories about negotiating and resolving issues with workers' unions regarding employee benefits. These positive news stories were a counter response by both Qantas and BHP to negative news, which prevented the returns on those days from falling below beyond the benchmark.
- Experiments 7 and 8 show the results of using technique ($T2$) for selecting negative news. This selection function resulted in negative (MCARs) as expected. No news stories on the days selected for these experiments were highly relevant to BHP and Qantas. Therefore the expected decline in returns wasn't very significant.
- MCAR values are affected by news topic filtration, as we can observe in experiment 2 and 3 for Qantas. News related to strikes had more impact than news about oil. For QANTAS, we can see that using no topic filter in experiment 1 gives better results than filtering by topic 'JOB' in experiment 3 and worse than filtering by

Table 5. Experiments results

Exp. No.	Sentiment Scores Statistics		End of Day Stock Returns Results			
	No. of extreme negative news $|Y|$	No. of distinct event days	Mean cumulative abnormal return (MCAR)	Precision weighted (CAAR)	Patell Z	Generalized sign Z
1	83	48	+2.29 %	2.22 %	+0.842	+0.706
2	7	7	+4.52 %	4.18 %	+2.166*	1.599$
3	20	12	+0.77 %	+1.25 %	+0.488	-0.332
4	132	98	-0.21 %	-0.20 %	-1.391$	-2.368**
5	7	7	+0.14 %	0.27 %	0.626	-1.112
6	14	10	-0.28 %	-0.29 %	-0.741	-1.829*
7	19	4	-0.12 %	-0.26 %	-0.476	+ 0.423
8	12	5	-0.51 %	-0.51 %	-1.699*	-2.020*
Mean	36.75	23.87	0.825 %	0.832 %	-0.023	-0.616

topic 'O' in experiment 2. The same applies when comparing experiments 4, 5 and 6 for BHP.

In calculating the MCAR values the window selected was (−200, + 200) days, which normalizes the returns over a long period of time. Therefore, window size is an important parameter; more experiments should be conducted on smaller windows to observe medium term MCARs. The results confirm days where positive news are at lowest have more effect on MCAR values. Considering negative news only without factoring positive news offsets the effect of negative news on the market.

4.4 Discussion

Based on the experiments a few points can be made:

- The idea behind proposing the Comparison Parameters Model (CPM) is to understand how context and sentiment parameters are interconnected and how they impact the market. CPM allows the user to set a context and filter news sentiment data by selecting attributes. The experiments prove that connecting news and market data relies on the technique used to select news.
- The choice of a sentiment scoring function is also important. Naively choosing the days in which there is a high negative score (as in function $T1$) does not work well as there could be positive news on the same day. Function $T2$ gives better results because it also accounts for positive news.
- CPM is supported by ADAGE services, which can be run independently or as part of a workflow. The workflow is presented to the user via a simple web based GUI as shown in Fig. 4. The TAVERNA workflow management system allows users to run

the workflows and reproduce the same results, as long as they run them using the same parameters. Since the market data used in the experiments is acquired "on-the-fly" from the original source, there is certainty that the evaluation results can be replicated.

The results overall demonstrate the importance of understanding, modeling and experimenting with a range of context and sentiment related parameters before using a sentiment dataset in a research or operational setting.

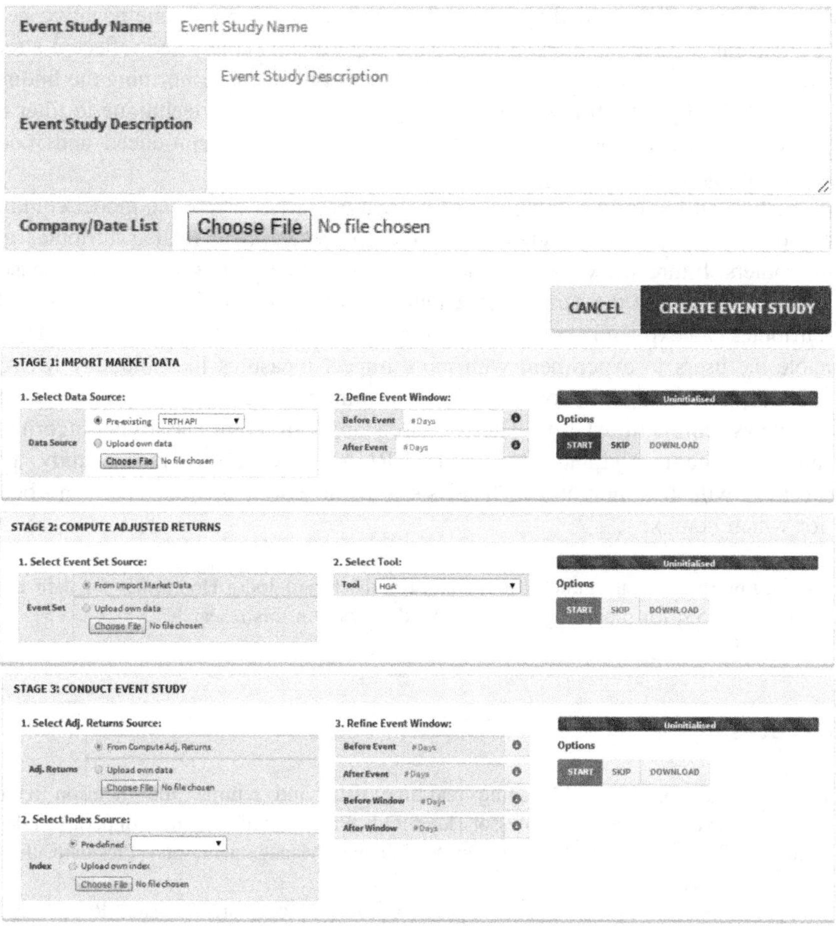

Fig. 4. Web-based GUI to enable execution of event studies workflow

5 Conclusion and Future Work

Extracting sentiment from text has been studied extensively and applied in various domains. The application of sentiment analysis in the finance domain has been of great interest to researchers, investors and financial entities. Many companies and research bodies read various kinds of news datasets {articles, blogs, tweets ....etc.} and automatically determine sentiment orientation and sentiment scores using text classification algorithms as a precursor to analyzing the impact on the market.

In this study we proposed a model called Comparison Parameters Model (CPM), which enables users to evaluate the effectiveness of news sentiment datasets in different contexts. To test our approach we used a sample from the Thomson Reuters News Analytics (TRNA) dataset and ran various experiments using extreme negative news for two Australian listed entities. Some of the experiments conducted reflected strong correlation between the negative news and the impact measure, confirming the findings of the literature. Significant results rely on devising an effective technique to filter the TRNA dataset. CPM enables experiments to be conducted, reproduced and model parameters to be saved and changed.

In the light of the results obtained, there are a few areas where the model could be improved. Firstly, the experiments considered some sentiment related attributes and ignored others, future work will conduct experiments using the same impact measure (i.e. daily MCAR) and the same TRNA dataset with different attributes, to see if the new attributes can explain impact more accurately. Secondly, we intend to extend CPM to enable the users to experiment with more impact measures like; intraday MCAR, volatility, liquidity and trade volume. We are also in the process of applying the model to other news sentiment datasets. These datasets apply different classifying algorithms the same news items read and classified by TRNA that were used in this study. This enhancement will shed light on which news sentiment scoring approach performs better and for which context.

Acknowledgments. We are grateful to Dennis Kundisch and Joerg Honnacker for their comments and Sirca [53] for providing access to the data used in this research.

References

1. Healy, A.D., Lo, A.W.: Managing real-time risks and returns: the thomson reuters newsscope event indices. In: Professor Hand, D.J., Professor of Statistics, Imperial College, London; Chief Scientific Advisor, Winton Capital Management; and President, Royal Statistical Society, 73
2. Moniz, A., Brar, G., Davis, C.: Have I got news for youMacQuarie Research Report (2009)
3. Al Shaikh, M.M., Prendinger, H., Ishizuka, M.: An analytical approach to assess sentiment of text. In: 10th International Conference on Computer and Information Technology, 2007 ICCIT 2007, pp. 1–6 (2007)
4. Antweiler, W., Frank, M.Z.: Is all that talk just noise? the information content of internet stock message boards. J. Finan. **59**(3), 1259–1294 (2004)

5. Azar, P.D.: Sentiment analysis in financial news (Doctoral dissertation, Harvard University) (2009)

6. Baker, M., Wurgler, J.: Investor sentiment and the cross section of stock returns. J. Finan. **61**(4), 1645–1680 (2006)

7. Barber, B.M., Odean, T.: All that glitters: The effect of attention and news on the buying behavior of individual and institutional investors. Rev. Finan. Stud. **21**(2), 785–818 (2008)

8. Beheshti, S., Venugopal, S., Ryu, S.H., Benatallah, B., Wang, W.: Big data and cross-document coreference resolution: Current state and future opportunities (2013). ArXiv Preprint arXiv:1311.3987

9. Bollen, J., Mao, H.: Twitter mood as a stock market predictor. Computer **44**(10), 0091–94 (2011)

10. Baker, B.H.: Types of media bias. Retrieved August, 2014. http://www.studentnewsdaily. com/types-of-media-bias/. (2013)

11. Cahan, R., Jussa, J., Luo, Y.: Breaking news: How to use news sentiment to pick stocks. Macquarie US Equity Research (2009)

12. Cambria, E., Schuller, B., Xia, Y., Havasi, C.: New avenues in opinion mining and sentiment analysis ieeexplore.ieee.org. (2013)

13. Cambria, E., Song, Y., Wang, H., Howard, N.: Semantic multi-dimensional scaling for open-domain sentiment analysis ieeexplore.ieee.org. (2013)

14. Cambria, E., Xia, Y., Hussain, A.: Affective common sense knowledge acquisition for sentiment analysis lrec.elra.info. (2012)

15. Carmelo Montalbano. (2014). How to measure stock returns. Retrieved Jan, 2014. http:// www.ehow.com/how_7811128_measure-stock-returns.html

16. Da, Z., Engelberg, J., Gao, P.: In search of attention. J. Finan. **66**(5), 1461–1499 (2011)

17. Das, S.R., Chen, M.Y.: Yahoo! for amazon: Sentiment extraction from small talk on the web. Manage. Sci. **53**(9), 1375–1388 (2007)

18. Dzielinski, M., Rieger, M.O., Talpsepp, T.: Volatility asymmetry, news, and private investors. The Handbook of News Analytics in Finance, pp. 255–270 (2011)

19. Fang, L., Peress, J.: Media coverage and the Cross section of stock returns. J. Finan. **64**(5), 2023–2052 (2009)

20. Hafez, P.: Detection of seasonality in newsflow. White Paper Available from RavenPack (2009)

21. Hagenau, M., Korczak, A., Neumann, D.: Buy on bad news, sell on good news: How insider trading analysis can benefit from textual analysis of corporate disclosures. In: Workshop on Information Systems and Economics (WISE 2012), Orlando, Florida, USA (2012)

22. Hirshleifer, D., Lim, S.S., Teoh, S.H.: Driven to distraction: Extraneous events and underreaction to earnings news. J. Finan. **64**(5), 2289–2325 (2009)

23. Investopedia (2014). Expected return. Retrieved Jan, 2014. http://www.investopedia.com/ terms/e/expectedreturn.asp

24. Investopedia. (2014). Retrieved Jan, 2014. http://www.investopedia.com

25. Jasny, B.R., Chin, G., Chong, L., Vignieri, S.: Data replication & reproducibility. again, and again, and again.... introduction. Science **334**(6060), 1225 (2011). (New York, N.Y.)

26. Jindal, N., Liu, B.: Identifying comparative sentences in text documents. In: Proceedings of the 29th Annual International ACM SIGIR Conference on Research and Development in Information Retrieval, pp. 244–251 (2006)

27. Joachims, T.: Making large scale SVM learning practical. Universität Dortmund (1999)

28. McCoy, C.J.: Understanding seasonality in search. Retrieved July, 2014. http://searchengine watch.com/article/2325080/Understanding-Seasonality-in-Search. (2014)

29. Kothari, S., Li, X., Short, J.E.: The effect of disclosures by management, analysts, and business press on cost of capital, return volatility, and analyst forecasts: A study using content analysis. Account. Rev. **84**(5), 1639–1670 (2009)

30. Leinweber, D.: Nerds on wall street. Math, Machines and Wired Markets (2009)

31. Zhang, L.: Sentiment analysis on twitter with stock price and significant keyword correlation. Retrieved Jan, 2014. http://apps.cs.utexas.edu/tech_reports/reports/tr/TR-2124.pdf. (2013)

32. Liu, B.: Sentiment analysis and opinion mining. Synth. Lect. Hum. Lang. Technol. **5**(1), 1–167 (2012)

33. Loughran, T., McDonald, B.: When is a liability not a liability? textual analysis, dictionaries, and 10 Ks. J. Finan. **66**(1), 35–65 (2011)

34. Lugmayr, A.: Predicting the future of investor sentiment with social media in stock exchange investments: A basic framework for the DAX performance index. In: Handbook of social media management, pp. 565–589. Springer, Heidelberg (2013)

35. Mitra, G., Mitra, L.: The handbook of news analytics in finance John Wiley & Sons. (2011)

36. Narayanan, R., Liu, B., & Choudhary, A. (2009). Sentiment analysis of conditional sentences. Proceedings of the 2009 Conference on Empirical Methods in Natural Language Processing: Volume 1-vol. 1, pp. 180–189

37. Nicholls, C., Song, F.: Comparison of feature selection methods for sentiment analysis. In: Advances in Artificial Intelligence, pp. 286–289. Springer, Berlin Heidelberg (2010)

38. O'Keefe, T., Koprinska, I.: Feature selection and weighting methods in sentiment analysis cs.otago.ac.nz. (2009)

39. Pang, B., Lee, L., Vaithyanathan, S.: Thumbs up?: Sentiment classification using machine learning techniques. In: Proceedings of the ACL-02 Conference on Empirical Methods in Natural Language Processing-vol. 10, pp. 79–86 (2002)

40. Pang, B., Lee, L.: A sentimental education: Sentiment analysis using subjectivity summarization based on minimum cuts. In: Proceedings of the 42nd Annual Meeting on (2004)

41. Peng, R.D.: Reproducible research in computational science. Science **334**(6060), 1226–1227 (2011). (New York, N.Y.)

42. Pink, G., Radford, W., Cannings, W., Naoum, A., Nothman, J., Tse, D., et al.: SYDNEY CMCRC at TAC 2013. In: Proceedings of the Text Analysis Conference (TAC2013) (2013)

43. Princeton University. WordNet: A lexical database for english. Retrieved June, 2014. http://wordnet.princeton.edu/. (2014)

44. Rabhi, F.A., Yao, L., Guabtni, A.: ADAGE: A framework for supporting user-driven ad-hoc data analysis processes. Computing **94**(6), 489–519 (2012)

45. Rasolofo, Y., Savoy, J.: Term proximity scoring for keyword-based retrieval systems. In: Sebastiani, F. (ed.) ECIR 2003. LNCS, vol. 2633, pp. 207–218. Springer, Heidelberg (2003)

46. RavenPack. RavenPack news scores user guideRavenPack (2010)

47. Robertson, C., Geva, S., Wolff, R.: What types of events provide the strongest evidence that the stock market is affected by company specific news? Proc. Fifth Australas. Conf. Data Min. Analytics **61**, 145–153 (2006)

48. Robertson, C.S., Rabhi, F.A., Peat, M.: A service-oriented approach towards real time financial news analysis. In: Consumer Information Systems (2011)

49. Schneider, K.: On word frequency information and negative evidence in naive bayes text classification. In: Advances in Natural Language Processing, pp. 474–485. Springer (2004)

50. Scott, J., Stumpp, M., Xu, P.: News, not trading volume, builds momentum. Finan. Anal. J. **46**, 45–54 (2003)

51. SenticNet (2014). Semantic based sentiment analysis. Retrieved April, 2014. http://sentic.net/api/en/concept/celebrate_special_occasion/

52. Siering, M.: "Boom" or "ruin"–does it make a difference? using text mining and sentiment analysis to support intraday investment decisions. In: 2012 45th Hawaii International Conference on System Science (HICSS), pp. 1050–1059 (2012)
53. Sirca (2014). Retrieved June, 2014. http://www.sirca.org.au/
54. Stanford named entity recognizer (NER). (27/08/2014). Retrieved May 2014, 2014. http://nlp.stanford.edu/software/CRF-NER.shtml
55. Taboada, M., Brooke, J., Tofiloski, M., Voll, K., Stede, M.: Lexicon-based methods for sentiment analysis. Computat. Linguist. **37**(2), 267–307 (2011)
56. Tetlock, P.C.: Giving content to investor sentiment: The role of media in the stock market. J. Finan. **62**(3), 1139–1168 (2007)
57. Tetlock, P.C., Saar Tsechansky, M., Macskassy, S.: More than words: Quantifying language to measure firms' fundamentals. J. Finan. **63**(3), 1437–1467 (2008)
58. Reuters, T.: (2013). OpenCalais product. Retrieved July, 2014. http://www.opencalais.com/
59. Reuters, T.: Thomson reuters news analyticsÂ. Retrieved Jan, 2014. http://thomsonreuters.com/products/financial-risk/01_255/news-analytics-product-brochure–oct-2010.pdf. (2010)
60. Turney, P.D.: Thumbs up or thumbs down?: Semantic orientation applied to unsupervised classification of reviews. In: Proceedings of the 40th Annual Meeting on Association for Computational Linguistics, pp. 417–424 (2002)
61. University of Sheffield. (2014). GATE projects. Retrieved Mar 2014, 2014. https://gate.ac.uk/projects.html
62. What is search volume index? (2013). Retrieved August, 2014. http://www.quora.com/What-is-Search-Volume-Index
63. Wiebe, J.M., Bruce, R.F., O'Hara, T.P.: Development and use of a gold-standard data set for subjectivity classifications. In: Proceedings of the 37th Annual Meeting of the Association for Computational Linguistics on Computational Linguistics, pp. 246–253 (1999)
64. BHP Billiton. BHP billiton. Retrieved September, 2014. http://www.bhpbilliton.com/home/Pages/default.aspx. (2014)
65. Qantas. Qantas. Retrieved September, 2014, from http://www.qantas.com.au/travel/airlines/home/au/en. (2014)
66. Australian Stock Exchange (ASX) All ordinaries index. Retrieved September, 2014. http://www.asx.com.au/listings/listing-IPO-on-ASX.htm. (2014)
67. Li, F.: Do Stock Market Investors Understand the Downside Risk Sentiment of Corporate Annual Reports (2007)
68. Minev, M., Schommer, C., Grammatikos, T.: News and stock markets: A survey on abnormal returns and prediction models (2012)
69. Nassirtoussi, A.K., Aghabozorgi, S., Wah, T.Y., Ngo, D.C.L.: Text mining for market prediction: A systematic review. Expert Syst. Appl. **41**(16), 7653–7670 (2014)
70. Reuters, T.: Thomson reuters news analytics. Retrieved February, 2015. http://thomsonreuters.com/content/dam/openweb/documents/pdf/tr-com-financial/news-analytics-product-brochure–oct-2010.pdf
71. Cowan Research LC, U. (2012). Eventus software. Retrieved February, 2015. http://www.eventstudy.com/index.html
72. Professor Carole Goble School of Computer Science at the University of Manchester, UK. Taverna workflow management system. Retrieved February, 2015. http://www.taverna.org.uk/

Finding Evidence of Irrational Exuberance
in the Oil Market

Antal Ratku[1], Stefan Feuerriegel[1,2]($\boxtimes$), Fethi A. Rabhi[2], and Dirk Neumann[1]

[1] Information Systems Research, University of Freiburg, Platz der Alten Synagoge,
79098 Freiburg, Germany
[2] School of Computer Science and Engineering, University of New South Wales,
Sydney 2052, Australia
stefan.feuerriegel@is.uni-freiburg.de

Abstract. The availability of novel information may significantly affect the evolution of asset prices. Nonetheless, investors are influenced not only by the quantitative facts but also by the textual content of news disclosures. In this paper, we examine whether news reception in the oil market is time-dependent using a rolling window regression. Our findings suggest that news reception does indeed have a significant effect on returns and we further find evidence for exaggerated news reception as it comes along with a feedback loop. Thus, we succeed in measuring the situation Shiller terms "irrational exuberance".

Keywords: Irrational exuberance · Information processing · Oil market · Rolling window regression · Sentiment analysis

1 Introduction

Due to recent technological advancements, today's investors have at their disposal inexpensive and quick access to information. When a novel information is released to the market, it can potentially reach a wide range of investors and triggers a corresponding price reaction. Assuming the so-called semi-strong form of market efficiency [12,13], this asset price reaction will occur shortly after a news disclosure. How markets react to news announcements has been the focus of many research publications (e. g. [6,7,9,29,33]) – all findings establish a relationship between the facts embedded in news releases and stock returns.

According to contemporary studies [2,24,35], investors are not only influenced by the quantitative content of news announcements, but also pay attention to their tone. Furthermore, their reaction is dependent on the economic environment – in some cases, they are highly receptive to optimistic news announcements, although this is not always so [33]. For example, when increasing asset prices yield positive returns, the news of these successes are quickly disseminated to the markets. This attracts more investors, which in turn increases prices further. These herding effects create positive *feedback loops* that fuel the development of speculative bubbles. According to Shiller [33], such eras of so-called

© Springer International Publishing Switzerland 2015
A. Lugmayr (Ed.): FinanceCom 2014, LNBIP 217, pp. 48–59, 2015.
DOI: 10.1007/978-3-319-28151-3_4

irrational exuberance end when the focus of debate can no longer be upbeat as before. As a consequence, he states that *"there are times when an audience is highly receptive to optimistic statements, and times when it is not"*. More precisely, when these bubbles burst, the falling asset prices launch the same reaction chain but in a reverse direction, leading to plummeting prices and considerable losses [1].

Following Shiller's argument, this paper investigates how news reception in the oil market changes over time. As a contribution, we find peaks in news reception around the fiscal year change 2008/09, in which investors were more receptive to news than in previous years. We interpret this spike as a negative feedback loop in the oil market and so regard it as an indication of irrational exuberance.

We choose the oil market for several reasons: most importantly because the oil market has drawn significant attention in the globalized world. With manufacturing businesses becoming highly dependent on oil, demand has literally exploded, reflected by the vast increase in traded oil futures, a total of 138.5 million contracts, each accounting for 1000 barrels in 2008.[1] Furthermore, oil demand is likely to grow in the future. According to the Organization of the Petroleum Exporting Countries, OPEC for short, estimated demand[2] will increase until the year 2035 by 20 million barrels a day. In recent years, oil markets have undergone extreme price peaks. As a consequence of both demand and price developments, the oil market has attracted many investors and is consequently subject to broad news coverage.

The remainder of this paper is structured as follows. In Sect. 2, we review previous research that links oil news and stock market reactions. To investigate these reactions, Sect. 3 describes both rolling window regression and so-called sentiment analysis to study news tone. By combining the two in Sect. 4, we study how news reception changes temporally, particularly with regard to irrational exuberance.

2   Related Work

In this section, we present related literature grouped into two categories. First, we collect studies that link oil news and stock market reactions. Second, we review literature that aim at detecting market overreactions, as well as irrational exuberance, in the context of news disclosure.

---

[1] CBS News. *Oil Trading's Powerful "Dark Markets"*. 2011. URL: http://www.cbsnews.com/2100-18564_162-4188620.html, accessed September 9, 2014.

[2] OPEC. *2013 World Oil Outlook*. URL: http://www.opec.org/opec_web/static_files_project/media/downloads/publications/WOO_2013.pdf, accessed September 9, 2014.

2.1   Linking Oil News and Stock Market Reaction

Information processing has been studied extensively in capital markets, whereas literature focusing on commodity markets is rare [37]. In the search for related literature, we came across only a few relevant references, which are as follows.

Several references perform event studies to analyze the impact of OPEC announcements on oil prices. For example, the informational efficiency of crude oil spot and futures markets is examined [11] with respect to these announcements. Furthermore, announcements from both OPEC official conferences and ministerial meetings have an effect [23] on major international crude. Similarly, oil prices react upon news announcements that disclose macroeconomic information [8,20]. All of these papers regard announcements as proxies for changes in fundamental variables (such as quotas) but this lies in contrast to analyzing the actual content of news.

When investigating content, news sentiment reveals a long-term effect [22] along with various (control) variables on crude oil prices. Similarly, empirical evidence shows that abnormal returns in oil markets can be explained to a large extent by news sentiment [16]. Additionally, the influence of news sentiment varies [15] across bullish and bearish market regimes and, according to [14], news causally influence abnormal returns.

2.2   Market Overreaction and Irrational Exuberance

While the previous paragraphs elaborate on the link between news and stock market returns, we now proceed to combine this link with irrationality; a combination which seems to be a nebulous concept. Irrationality attracts significant attention from the domain of behavioral finance. For instance, financial markets show excess volatility to new information [32], as well as overreaction. Similarly, a parsimonious model of investor sentiment [3] shows that news can entail both over- and underreaction of stock prices.

Without doubt, media has an outstanding importance in financial markets globally. Therefore, it is reasonable not only to study news reception but, assuming that markets are not efficient, it is also intriguing to examine under- and overreaction in prices due to news releases. There are attempts, e. g. [30], to test for explosive behaviors in a recursive fashion, but this approach does not incorporate the news component. In contrast, the news component is included in several publications [15,34,36] which study news tone in the shed of the boom and bust phases. However, we are not aware of any previous work that aims at actually measuring heightened states of news reception. That is why we propose a novel ansatz to study feedback loops, which we evaluate using the oil market as an example.

3   Research Methodology

This section introduces our research methodology: first, we show how to compute daily sentiment values. Second, we present the event study methodology to retrieve abnormal returns. Both are combined in a rolling window regression to analyze time-varying news reception.

3.1 Sentiment Analysis

Methods that use the textual representation of documents to measure the positivity and negativity of the content are referred to as opinion mining or *sentiment analysis*. Before we perform the sentiment analysis, we carry out several operations during a preprocessing phase [16], namely, tokenization, negation scope detection [31], stop word removal and stemming. Then, we measure sentiment according to the Net-Optimism metric [10], utilizing Henry's Finance-Specific Dictionary [18]. The Net-Optimism metric $S(t)$ is applied to all news originating from a full day t. It is calculated as the difference between the number of positive $W_{pos}(A)$ and negative $W_{neg}(A)$ words divided by the total number of words $W_{tot}(A)$ in each announcement A. Thus, Net-Optimism $S(t)$ and the standardized counterpart are defined by

$$S(t) = \frac{\sum_A W_{pos}(A) - W_{neg}(A)}{\sum_A W_{tot}(A)} \text{ and } S^*(t) = \frac{S(t) - \mu}{\sigma} \in (-\infty, +\infty) \qquad (1)$$

which is scaled to feature a zero mean and a standard deviation of one.

3.2 Abnormal Returns

A common way to study the effects of certain events on stock or commodity prices is to use an event study methodology [21, 26]. When using such methods, we first have to predict a *normal return* in the absence of such an event. Afterwards, we calculate the *abnormal return* as the difference between the actual and the normal return. In our research, the event of interest consists of all daily oil-related announcements from the news corpus. We decided to aggregate daily news disclosures, since we are provided with daily financial market data.

We estimate the normal return by the so-called *market model*, which assumes a stable linear relation [26] between the market return $R_m(t)$ and the normal return $R(t)$. More precisely, the market model is described as

$$R(t) = \alpha + \beta R_m(t) + \varepsilon_t \quad \forall t \in T , \qquad (2)$$

where ε_t is a zero mean disturbance term. We model the market return $R_m(t)$ using a commodity index, namely, the Dow Jones-UBS Commodity Index [11], along with an event window T of 10 trading days prior to the event. We then determine the abnormal return of an event that occurs in period τ by

$$AR(\tau) = R(\tau) - \alpha - \beta R_m(\tau) . \qquad (3)$$

3.3 Rolling Window Regression

Using a single linear regression to describe a relationship between data collected over a long period has a major drawback: such a method does not allow for time-dependent changes in the underlying model. In the financial world, one might expect that at different times, certain factors influence investor behavior in a different way. As a remedy [27], such dynamics can be integrated by using *rolling window regressions*.

In our paper, one of the main interests is to investigate whether the effect of news sentiment is time-dependent; a risk factor, which may not be constant over time [4]. The motivation behind this question is that in different time periods the news sentiment may have a different effect on crude oil prices. To account for this additional freedom, we use the aforementioned rolling window regression. As such, we take a sub-sample of 80 consecutive business days (approximately 4 months) and calculate the influence of news sentiment in this sub-sample. Afterwards, we iteratively slide forward this 80 day window by one day and estimate the new coefficients. In the end, we receive a time series of coefficients, which reveal how the partial effect of sentiment and other variables on abnormal returns changes over time.

4 Investigating Irrational Exuberance in Oil Markets

Having discussed the methods that underly our research, we apply these in order to investigate news reception in oil markets. First, we specify our datasets, including the news corpus and, second, describe the regression design of our confirmatory analysis, i.e. how news sentiment drives oil prices. Third, we observe that news absorption changes over time and then interpret this as evidence of a (negative) feedback loop, i.e. irrational exuberance.

4.1 Datasets

All news originates from the *Thomson Reuters News Archive* for Machine Readable News. We choose this source of information, since the Thomson Reuters transmits independent, third-party announcements with shorter delay than printed media [25,28] and can thus be used to evaluate stock market reactions. All announcements provided by Reuters are extracted from between January 6, 2004 until May 31, 2012. Moreover, this information source enables us to effectively collect all the crude oil related announcements in the English language, while automatically omitting personal alerts or opinions, which might have a limited or even difficult to interpret information content. This is achieved by applying a set of filter criteria [14]. All in all, this gives a total of 307,430 announcements related to crude oil.

News sentiment can affect daily WTI crude oil prices $P(t)$. Apparently, WTI crude oil prices are a common choice [5,8,20] in research that studies oil markets since it acts as the benchmark U.S. price. In addition, we integrate several fundamentals as control variables, consistent with previous research [19,22]. These are as follows: U.S. interest rate $r(t)$, U.S. Dollar/Euro exchange rate $FX(t)$, level $IM(t)$ of oil imports (in million barrel), total open interest $OI(t)$ in crude oil future contracts (in million), gold price $G(t)$ (London, afternoon fixing), S&P 500 index $SP(t)$ (additionally included). All data spanning the time frame January 6, 2004 until May 31, 2012 originates from Thomson Reuters Datastream. We only include business days, giving a total of 2108 observations for each daily time series.

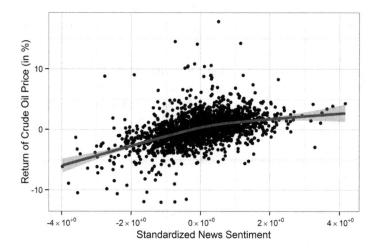

Fig. 1. GAM (generalized additive model) trend line showing relationship between standardized news sentiment and stock market returns.

The relationship of news sentiment and corresponding stock market returns is depicted in Fig. 1. This diagram features a trend line from a so-called generalized additive model (GAM), in which the linear predictor depends linearly on unknown smooth functions of some predictor variables. From this GAM trend line, we can identify a visible relationship between the sentiment variable and stock market returns.

4.2   Confirmatory Analysis: Measuring Average News Reception

In this section, we present our regression design which investigates investor reaction to the news tone. For this purpose, we use an event study methodology, in which our dependent variable $AR_{\log}(t)$ is the abnormal log-return of crude oil prices corresponding to the abovementioned abnormal return. The key explanatory variable in our design is the standardized news sentiment $S^*(t)$. Finally, we include control variables according to [19,22] and account for seasonal effects by using monthly dummy variables $D_i(t)$. Altogether, our regression design is given by

$$AR_{\log}(t) = \beta_0 + \beta_1\, S^*(t) + \beta_2\, r_{\log}(t) + \beta_3\, FX_{\log}(t) + \beta_4\, IM(t)$$
$$+ \beta_5\, OI(t) + \beta_6\, G_{\log}(t) + \beta_7\, SP_{\log}(t) + \sum_i \gamma_i\, D_i(t) + \varepsilon(t), \qquad (4)$$

where $r_{\log}(t)$, $FX_{\log}(t)$, $G_{\log}(t)$ and $SP_{\log}(t)$ denote log-returns. To account for the distorting effect of extreme outliers, we remove them at both ends at the 0.05 % level.

We tested for autocorrelation, constant variance, serial correlation and normally distributed residuals at the 0.001 % level to ensure that the results are not confounded. When checking Variance Inflation Factors, we also see no indication of multicollinearity. Independence across announcements is given as long as all news stories are entirely novel and not based on an interrelated course of events. However, after analyzing our regression results with the Goldfeld-Quandt test, a significant level of heteroskedasticity is revealed. Under the assumption that returns are jointly multivariate normal, as well as independently and identically distributed through time, the model can be estimated using a heteroskedasticity-corrected estimator. Thus, we only present heteroskedasticity-robust t-statistics.

Table 1. Confirmatory analysis measuring how tone in oil-related news influences abnormal log-returns of crude oil.

Variable		(1)	(2)	(3)	(4)	(5)	(6)	(7)
$S^*(t)$	News Sentiment	1.223***	1.225***	1.179***	1.180***	1.183***	1.174***	1.062***
		(17.868)	(17.887)	(17.013)	(17.026)	(17.076)	(16.844)	(15.086)
$r_{\log}(t)$	U. S. Interest Rate		-0.018	-0.020	-0.021	−0.127**	−0.127**	−0.114*
			(-1.306)	(-1.357)	(-1.440)	(-2.735)	(-2.739)	(-2.506)
$FX_{\log}(t)$	\$/€ Exch. Rate			0.240	0.241	0.235	0.205	0.112
				(1.681)	(1.689)	(1.645)	(1.340)	(0.715)
$IM(t)$	Oil Imports				0.003	0.003	0.003	0.001
					(0.464)	(0.598)	(0.608)	(0.171)
$OI(t)$	Oil Futures					−4.093*	−4.098*	−3.563*
						(-2.37)	(-2.37)	(-2.121)
$G_{\log}(t)$	Gold Price						0.049	0.089
							(0.675)	(1.285)
$SP_{\log}(t)$	S&P 500 Index							0.340***
								(5.516)
Intercept β_0		0.646**	0.277	0.266	-0.480	1.832	1.809	2.105
		(2.666)	(0.651)	(0.609)	(-0.288)	(0.925)	(0.913)	(1.092)
Adjusted R^2		0.139	0.139	0.142	0.141	0.144	0.143	0.175
AIC		9687.458	9688.696	9681.800	9683.484	9679.237	9680.428	9601.457
BIC		10264.115	10271.006	10269.763	10277.101	10278.508	10285.352	10212.035

Stated: OLS coefficients, heteroskedasticity-robust t-statistics in parenthesis
Dummies: monthly; Obs.: 2108; Significance: *** 0.001, ** 0.01, * 0.05

The regression results are presented in Table 1. Accordingly, we observe that the sentiment variable is highly significant. The corresponding t-statistic of more than 15 and the positivity of the coefficient suggest that our results are robust and stable, and coincide with *prior* assumptions that negative news affects returns negatively and vice versa. Hence, the news reception coefficient of 1.062 signifies that a one standard deviation increase in the sentiment metric explains an economically significant 6.2 % increase in abnormal log-returns.

In addition to the sentiment values, the S&P 500 index is highly significant, while the U. S. interest rate and the open interest in crude oil futures are significant at a lower level. The other control variables do not contribute significantly to the explanation of abnormal returns. According to the adjusted R^2, AIC and BIC measures, we observe that regression design (7) is the most useful in explaining the oil market returns. The corresponding adjusted R^2 of 0.175 shows that the absorption of news disclosures plays a major role in the evolution of the oil price.

4.3 Time-Varying News Reception as an Indicator for Irrational Exuberance

In Sect. 4.2, we provided evidence that news reception is an essential factor in explaining abnormal returns of oil prices. However, we might suppose that this effect changes over time. This motivates our research regarding how news reception varies temporally.

To answer this question, we use a rolling window regression on the underlying data. The regression design is similar to the previous one presented in Eq. (4); however, the results are obtained from evaluating consecutive subsets of the underlying data, as described in Sect. 3.3, which introduces the concept of rolling window regressions. This design provides a suitable way to investigate the time-dependence of the explanatory variables and, as a result, helps to answer the question of whether the effect of news reception fluctuates over time.

The results of the rolling window regression are presented in Fig. 2. The time series at the top denotes the nominal crude oil price, followed by the cumulative standardized news sentiment. After evaluating our model across all rolling regression windows, we also include both the sentiment coefficients and their t-statistics. Moreover, we indicate the beginning of the third quarter of 2008 and the end of the first quarter of 2009 by vertical dashed lines in order to mark the most severe period of the financial crisis according to our news sentiment coefficient $\beta_1(t)$. Finally, the three horizontal lines in the sentiment coefficient graph represent the news reception coefficient from the confirmatory analysis, as well as the plus/minus three standard deviation confidence interval.

Our results strongly suggest that the effect of news reception is not constant over time, since we observe considerable variance in the sentiment coefficients $\beta_1(t)$. This suggests that, during the time period under study, there are times when investors pay more attention to news announcements, whereas sometimes news reception is barely significant. Furthermore, we observe that the t-statistic corresponding to the sentiment coefficients is also not constant over time. It is worth noting that we studied the behavior of all other coefficients, as well as their t-statistics. We found that, although they are also not constant over time, their variance is considerably smaller than that of news reception. In addition, we find spikes in the sentiment coefficient which might reasonably be attributed to political and economic changes, such as the beginning of the Iraq war in the spring of 2003, or the financial crisis in the years 2008 and 2009.

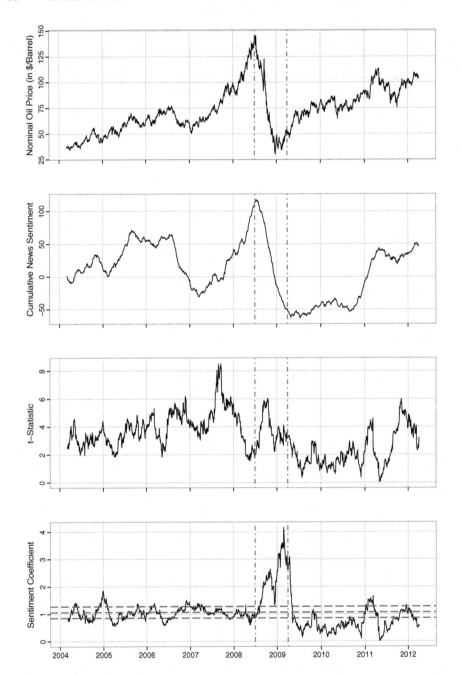

Fig. 2. Nominal crude oil price (1st plot) and cumulative news sentiment (2nd), together with heteroskedasticity-robust t-statistics (3rd) and their corresponding sentiment coefficients (4th). We further indicate the period from 2007Q3 until 2008Q1, and the confirmatory analysis sentiment coefficient together with a three standard deviation confidence interval.

We analyzed the behavior of sentiment coefficients within and outside the period from 2008Q3 until 2009Q1. When testing the difference, both the Bartlett test and the Levene's test suggest that the variance in news reception coefficients is not homogeneous. This outcome provides strong evidence that the underlying two periods, from which the coefficients are calculated, are not identical. In fact, the period 2008Q3 until 2009Q1 features an average sentiment coefficient of 2.517, while it drops to only 0.993 outside of this period. Similarly, the corresponding standard deviations decrease from 0.805 down to 0.377. This effect is robust, even when varying the size of the regression window.

Overall, we observe a considerable difference in news reception. This agrees with the *"underlying story of investors overreacting to news and of the feedback of price increases leading to further price increases [which] often tends to get lost"* [33]. Altogether, we cannot reasonably assume that our model's parameters remain constant but instead vary throughout the entire sample. Accordingly, this instability is captured by our rolling window estimates. This provides evidence of a (negative) feedback loop, i. e. irrational exuberance. The above results are furthermore consistent with contemporary research findings that investors tend to react more strongly to news when primed for negative mood states [17].

5   Conclusion and Outlook

Alan Greenspan once coined the phrase *irrational exuberance* as a warning that the market during the dot-com bubble was overvalued, as prices had unduly escalated asset values. Assuming overconfidence in the market and in predicted future prices, a group of investors can dominate the market, making their predictions (at least for some time) self-fulfilling. Such a self-fulfilling *feedback loop* is limited up to the point at which the fundamental values reveal that initial expectations were too optimistic and, afterwards, the market developments reverse. The term *irrational exuberance*, following Shiller's book [33] with the same name, is now typically used to describe a heightened state of speculative mania; this frequently occurs alongside differences in receptiveness to the news.

In this paper, we analyzed the processing of news in oil markets. We thus extracted the (subjective) tone from oil news and linked it to abnormal log-returns of crude oil. One standard deviation increase in the sentiment measure is positively linked to an increase in abnormal log-returns by an economically significant 6.2 %. Furthermore, we adopted a rolling window regression to examine the time-dependent behavior of news reception and observed a considerable spike in news reception during the fiscal year change 2008/09, in which investors paid more attention and more strongly absorbed news. We interpret this spike as a (negative) feedback loop in an attempt to find evidence of irrational exuberance in the oil market.

Our work opens avenues for further research questions. One of the most intriguing research directions is to model the behavior of the sentiment coefficients with dynamic linear models instead of with rolling-window regressions. As an alternative, this approach keeps the coefficients of all control variables constant. This assumption is supported by our research results, which show that the coefficients of the control variables have a considerably smaller variance than those of the sentiment values. Furthermore, to validate the robustness of our findings, we intend to augment this methodology to other commodity markets, such as gold, or even capital markets.

References

1. Akerlof, G.A., Shiller, R.J.: Animal Spirits: How Human Psychology Drives the Economy, and Why It Matters for Global Capitalism. Princeton University Press, Princeton (2010)
2. Antweiler, W., Frank, M.Z.: Is all that talk just noise? The information content of internet stock message boards. J. Finance **59**(3), 1259–1294 (2004)
3. Barberis, N., Shleifer, A., Vishny, R.: A model of investor sentiment. J. Financial Econ. **49**(3), 307–343 (1998)
4. Basher, S.A., Sadorsky, P.: Oil price risk and emerging stock markets. Glob. Finance J. **17**(2), 224–251 (2006)
5. Bencivenga, C., D'Ecclesia, R.L., Triulzi, U.: Oil prices and the financial crisis. RMS **6**(3), 227–238 (2012)
6. Bohn, N., Rabhi, F.A., Kundisch, D., Yao, L., Mutter, T.: Towards automated event studies using high frequency news and trading data. In: Rabhi, F.A., Gomber, P. (eds.) FinanceCom 2012. LNBIP, vol. 135, pp. 20–41. Springer, Heidelberg (2013)
7. Cenesizoglu, T.: The reaction of stock returns to news about fundamentals. Manage. Sci. **61**(5), 1072–1093 (2015)
8. Chatrath, A., Miao, H., Ramchander, S.: Does the price of crude oil respond to macroeconomic news? J. Futures Markets **32**(6), 536–559 (2012)
9. Cutler, D.M., Poterba, J.M., Summers, L.H.: What moves stock prices? J. Portfolio Manag. **15**(3), 4–12 (1989)
10. Demers, E., Vega, C.: Soft information in earnings announcements: news or noise? In: International Finance Discussion Papers (2010)
11. Demirer, R., Kutan, A.M.: The behavior of crude oil spot and futures prices around OPEC and SPR announcements: an event study perspective. Energy Econ. **32**(6), 1467–1476 (2010)
12. Fama, E.F.: Efficient capital markets: a review of theory and empirical work. J. Finance **25**(2), 383–417 (1970)
13. Fama, E.F.: The behavior of stock-market prices. J. Bus. **38**(1), 34–105 (1965)
14. Feuerriegel, S., Heitzmann, S.F., Neumann, D.: Do investors read too much into news? How news sentiment causes price formation. In: 48th Hawaii International Conference on System Sciences (HICSS) (2015)
15. Feuerriegel, S., Lampe, M.W., Neumann, D.: News processing during speculative bubbles: evidence from the oil market. In: 47th Hawaii International Conference on System Sciences (HICSS) (2014)
16. Feuerriegel, S., Neumann, D.: News or noise? How news drives commodity prices. In: Proceedings of the International Conference on Information Systems (ICIS 2013). Association for Information Systems (2013)
17. Garcia, D.: Sentiment during recessions. J. Finance **68**(3), 1267–1300 (2013)
18. Henry, E.: Are investors influenced by how earnings press releases are written? J. Bus. Commun. **45**(4), 363–407 (2008)

19. Kilian, L.: Not all oil price shocks are alike: disentangling demand and supply shocks in the crude oil market. Am. Econ. Rev. **99**(3), 1053–1069 (2009)
20. Kilian, L., Vega, C.: Do energy prices respond to U.S. macroeconomic news? A test of the hypothesis of predetermined energy prices. Rev. Econ. Statistics **93**(2), 660–671 (2011)
21. Konchitchki, Y., O'Leary, D.E.: Event study methodologies in information systems research. Int. J. Account. Inf. Syst. **12**(2), 99–115 (2011)
22. Lechthaler, F., Leinert, L.: Moody Oil-What is Driving the Crude Oil Price?. Eidgenössische Technische Hochschule Zürich, CER-ETH-Center of Economic Research, ETH Zurich (2012)
23. Lin, S.X., Tamvakis, M.: OPEC announcements and their effects on crude oil prices. Energy Policy **38**(2), 1010–1016 (2010)
24. Loughran, T., McDonald, B.: When is a liability not a liability? Textual analysis, dictionaries, and 10-Ks. J. Finance **66**(1), 35–65 (2011)
25. MacGregor, P.: International news agencies: global eyes that never blink. In: Fowler-Watt, K., Allan, S. (eds.) Journalism, pp. 35–63. Centre for Journalism & Communication Research, Bournemouth University (2013)
26. MacKinlay, A.C.: Event studies in economics and finance. J. Econ. Lit. **35**(1), 13–39 (1997)
27. Meyer, R.A.: Estimating coefficients that change over time. Int. Econ. Rev. **13**(3), 705 (1972)
28. Paterson, C.: International news on the internet: why more is less. Ethical Space: Int. J. Commun. Ethics **4**(1/2), 57–66 (2007)
29. Pearce, D.K., Vance, R.V.: Stock prices and economic news. J. Bus. **58**(1), 49–67 (1985)
30. Phillips, P.C.B., Wu, Y., Yu, J.: Explosive behavior in the 1990s NASDAQ: when did exuberance escalate asset values? Int. Econ. Rev. **52**(1), 201–226 (2011)
31. Pröllochs, N., Feuerriegel, S., Neumann, D.: Enhancing sentiment analysis of financial news by detecting negation scopes. In: 48th Hawaii International Conference on System Sciences (HICSS) (2015)
32. Shiller, R.J.: Do stock prices move too much to be justified by subsequent changes in dividends? Am. Econ. Rev. **71**(3), 421–436 (1981)
33. Shiller, R.J.: Irrational Exuberance, 2nd edn. Princeton University Press, Princeton (2005)
34. Soo, C.: Quantifying Animal Spirits: News Media and Sentiment in the Housing Market (2013)
35. Tetlock, P.C.: Giving content to investor sentiment: the role of media in the stock market. J. Finance **62**(3), 1139–1168 (2007)
36. Walker, C.B.: Housing booms and media coverage. Appl. Econ. **46**(32), 3954–3967 (2014)
37. Wex, F., Widder, N., Liebmann, M., Neumann, D.: Early warning of impending oil crises using the predictive power of online news stories. In: 47th Hawaii International Conference on System Sciences (HICSS), pp. 1512–1521 (2014)

Validating an Incremental Rule Management Approach for Financial Market Data Pre-processing

Weisi Chen[✉] and Fethi A. Rabhi

School of Computer Science and Engineering,
University of New South Wales, Sydney 2052, Australia
chenw@cse.unsw.edu.au, f.rabhi@unsw.edu.au

Abstract. Driven by the growth and availability of vast amounts of financial market data, financial studies are becoming increasingly of interest to finance researchers. However, financial market data is normally huge in amount and with data quality issues especially time-related ones, which renders it extremely difficult to generate reliable results and get interesting insights. Data pre-processing is hence necessary to control data quality and have raw data standardised, which is often achieved by using bespoke or commercial tools. In this paper, we first define *ACTER* criteria (automatability, customisability, time-handleability, evolvability and repeatability) to assess a financial market data pre-processing system. Then we update our previously proposed system (*EP-RDR*), which uses an incremental rule management approach for building and conducting user-driven event data analysis, with some new features to make it more suitable for financial market data pre-processing. Finally, we apply the *ACTER* criteria on an *EP-RDR* prototype as well as some other existing tools in the context of two real-life financial study scenarios to compare the desirability of these tools for financial market data pre-processing.

Keywords: Rule management · Financial market data · Data pre-processing · Data quality

1 Introduction

Driven by the growth and availability of vast amounts of financial market data, financial studies are becoming increasingly more data intensive. In financial studies, researchers conduct data analysis by themselves in order to extract useful information, e.g. to explore the characteristics or the trend of changes in the data [1]. Prior to conducting any meaningful financial study, they expend a lot of effort in data collecting and pre-processing (also known as data preparation). Since data collecting is normally loosely controlled and many data quality issues such as missing data, duplicates and inconsistencies may exist, data pre-processing is an indispensible phase where researchers have to refine datasets by detecting and managing these data quality issues, and standardise the data to facilitate further processing and analysis. For example, before carrying out an event study [2] using a software tool (e.g. Eventus [3]), the researcher needs to first download the raw company stock data, and pre-process the

© Springer International Publishing Switzerland 2015
A. Lugmayr (Ed.): FinanceCom 2014, LNBIP 217, pp. 60–78, 2015.
DOI: 10.1007/978-3-319-28151-3_5

dataset, i.e. cleansing the data and calculating returns (see Fig. 1). If the data pre-processing is not done properly, the data analysis will end up with errors or unreasonable and unreliable results.

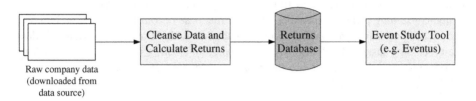

Fig. 1. Example of Data Pre-processing (for Event Studies).

In this paper, we will:

- propose a list of criteria for a desirable financial market data pre-processing system;
- update and apply our previous work to financial market data pre-processing; *and*
- validate our updated approach as well as some other tools.

The rest of the paper is organised as follows. In Sect. 2, we describe the background of the problem and suggest the criteria for a desirable financial market data pre-processing system. In Sect. 3, we review and update our previous work with some new features and finally a more suitable financial market data pre-processing system is proposed. Section 4 describes our experimental settings (i.e. what datasets to be used and how the rule sets will be). In Sect. 5, we discuss the result of our experiments. Section 6 concludes the paper.

2   Background and Related Work

Most financial market data can be categorised as event data , which denotes the data recording event occurrences with a timestamp, such as financial trades, banking transactions, news reports, etc. Financial market data has some characteristics of event data that render it hard to be processed:

- Time-based: Financial market data often has a temporal axis in the data schema. To be precise, every record is affixed with a timestamp.
- High flow rate and huge volume: Normally, new financial market data is continuously coming in to guarantee the timeliness of the data. Often, financial market data records are generated and stored in huge volumes, containing data for years. Some also come in high frequency, so even a dataset containing a day s records can be very huge.

Currently, to accomplish pre-processing tasks on financial market data, finance researchers have to rely on IT experts either to implement the processing rules as a bespoke program or to customise an existing software tools according to their processing rules.

However, a challenge is that in real-world financial market data pre-processing, rules are never perfect as there are always exceptions against existing rules, so the underlying data processing logic (also referred to as rules) may change over time to take new cases into account; thus finance researchers need to communicate their new requirements to IT experts all the time so IT experts can then update the rules, which is a time-consuming process especially when the rule base becomes huge in size. Figure 2 shows how a finance researcher could collaborate with IT experts to conduct data pre-processing tasks. More seriously, any change in existing rules will pose a risk of introducing more mistakes due to the possible corruption of the rule base [4].

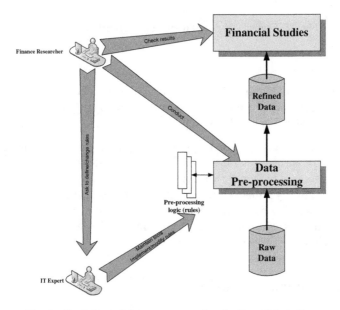

Fig. 2. Evolution of data pre-processing for financial studies.

Based on our experience working with finance researchers and literature, we have defined *ACTER* criteria to assist finance researchers to access and select a desirable tool for financial market data pre-processing:

- Automation (A) – Can all the financial market data pre-processing rules run automatically?
- Customisation (C) – Can the system be customised according to financial researchers' needs?
- Time handling (T) – Is the system capable to address time-related issues in financial market data?
- Evolution (E)– Are finance researchers able to evolve the system without IT experts involved?
- Repeatability (R) – Is the process still repeatable even after any update on the system (e.g. changes on processing rules, etc)?

Existing solutions for financial data pre-processing fall into two major categories: data pre-processing/cleansing in general and event processing. Unfortunately, literature suggests that there is no perfect solution which meets all the criteria listed above:

A vast variety of data pre-processing tools are available, either free or commercial. The common method in these tools is to split the cleansing process into several steps including auditing, parsing, standardisation, scrubbing, de-duplicating, integration, etc. [5]. Commercial tools (e.g. [6, 7]) are not very suitable for finance researchers because most of them are rather costly and not open to the public [8]. In terms of free tools, a typical and popular one is OpenRefine [9], which enables users to explore, normalise and clean up datasets by importing data, faceting, clustering to handle inconsistencies, and calling remote APIs to enrich data. It is powerful and flexible, and users can customise the tool to their own needs as long as the issues are general and not very complicated. Another advantage is that users can save their pre-processing rules in JSON format and apply them to similar datasets. However, more complicated data quality issues such as time-related ones involving complex event patterns in financial market data cannot be effectively addressed because the tool does not facilitate event pattern detection.

The second category is event processing systems (EPSs), which are dedicated platforms that perform operations on event data, including reading, filtering, transforming and generating events and consuming events [10]. Event processing logic is expressed by event processing languages (EPLs), such as Esper [11], Drools Fusion [12], Apama [13] and EventSwarm [14]. While EPSs are fairly good at handling time-related issues by way of enabling event pattern detection, to apply them directly to financial market data pre-processing is still challenging. First of all, learning to use an EPS is by no means an easy task; thus it is very challenging for non-IT researchers to define their own pre-processing rules directly using event processing languages. Furthermore, underlying EPLs all have advantages and disadvantages that reflect the usual tradeoffs between simplicity and expressiveness, so whatever EPL/EPS the finance user is able to use, there are always limitations, and switching is normally troublesome due to a lack of standard in EPS interfaces and EPLs. Last but not least, in present EPSs, rule sets are normally very simple and users are not able to evolve the pre-processing rule base effectively. Luckham has claimed that managing large sets of event processing rules in an EPS has not yet been effectively tackled [15] but most efforts in the event processing area are focusing on operational issues, e.g. event processing language expressiveness and performance [16].

We have previously proposed an architecture called EP-RDR that uses an incremental rule management approach for building and conducting user-driven event data analysis [17]. Its two main components are a Ripple-Down Rule (RDR) engine which enables the user to add a new rule only when they inspect an incorrect action, preventing the existing rule base from corruption; and an event pattern detection as a service (EPDaaS) which can interface with any event processing system (EPS) that can handle time-related issues quite well. However, the system did not take repeatability into account so every time the rule base is updated, previous data processing cannot be repeated. Additionally, the system has not been well validated.

In the rest of the paper, we will extend our previous work to make it satisfy all the criteria so that it is more suitable for financial market data pre-processing; and then validate the new system along with some other existing tools.

3   Updated System for Financial Market Data Pre-processing

3.1   EP-RDR for Financial Market Data Pre-processing

The architecture we proposed facilitates incremental event processing rule definition, which is desirable for system evolution, more precisely to eliminate rule rebuilding for financial market data pre-processing, to enhance the reuse of existing rules, to keep track of changes, to simplify the rule management process, and to avoid rule base collapse when the rule base gets big. It enables finance researchers to manage rules, define simple patterns or build patterns upon existing ones for financial market data with timestamps (i.e. event data). In addition, the platform can be incrementally enhanced by finance users. In this case, IT experts will only play one role in the data analysis process: to define and deploy complex event patterns.

Figure 3 shows how the architecture will fit into an entire financial study process. The two core components in the architecture are a rule-based system and an event pattern detection as a service (EPDaaS). In order to achieve incremental definition of rules based on the presence of event patterns each situation in financial market data is represented as an event pattern in a rule and eliminate clashes, we utilise Ripple-Down Rules (RDR) as the rule-based framework to route the event processing logic, because it has been proven to be capable to organise and maintain rule bases more effectively [18]. Unlike other rule management systems, RDR is an error-driven, incremental rule acquisition framework, which enables finance researchers to evolve the system solely by themselves and eliminates the risk of corrupting the rule base because all existing rules are never changed, which reserve the existing decision logic of the event processing. When errors are inspected by the user, RDR allows capturing the characteristic of the new case as an exception, and add a new rule to quickly recover the degraded performance. The case that prompted the addition of a rule is called a cornerstone case, which is stored along with the rule and is used to be compared with new cases by the finance researchers. It has been proved that the whole processing of adding a rule including checking cornerstone cases takes only a couple of minutes [19].

The role of the EPDaaS component is to detect pattern occurrences so as to address time-related issues. The EPDaaS component has a service interface that has the capability to invoke any underlying EPS (using any EPL). When invoked with an event pattern type and a reference to a dataset, EPDaaS will select one available/suitable EPS, run the corresponding EPL code and finally return occurrences of the particular pattern in this dataset, or abstractions or aggregations of these occurrences.

The architecture provides the link between the RDR component and the EPDaaS component, i.e. the RDR component sends a request to detect an event pattern, and the EPDaaS responds with event pattern occurrences back to the RDR. Finally, RDR will generate a list of actions on the original dataset, which will be inspected by the finance researcher. One of the advantages of this architecture is that for different event data

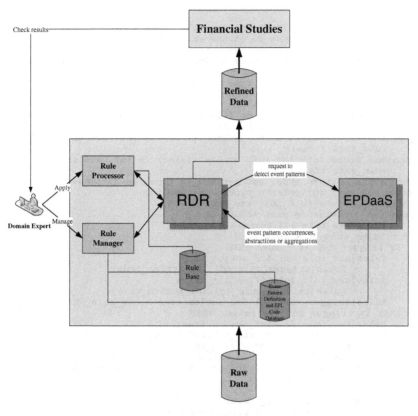

Fig. 3. Proposed EP-RDR architecture

analysis, the only things that have to be changed are the rule set and the choice of the EPS invoked by the EPDaaS component; the RDR component, however, does not have to be changed. IT experts are not involved in rule management but managing the EPL code in the database.

3.2 New Features to Enhance the System

Generally, the structure of a rule in this architecture is:

    If

        / an **event pattern** occurs*/*
        the number of occurrences >= 0;

    Then

        case action;
        inference action: *go to rule a*;

    Else

        inference action: *go to rule b*;

```
BEGIN ADD_RULE
  /** new_rule_id: the ID of the new rule to be added
   ** trigger_rule_id: the ID of the existing rule that is related to
      the inspected incorrect action
   ** trigger_inf: the predicate to denote whether the true inf. action
      or the false inf. action triggered the addition of the new rule
   ** rule_size: the current size of the rule set
  */
  new_rule_id = rule_size + 1;
  Add inf. action for rule_size (true) & inf. action for rule_size
      (false) in the rule base schema;
  Copy and store existing inf. action (true) in inf. action for
      rule_size (true);
  Copy and store existing inf. action (false) in inf. action for
      rule_size (false);
  Define the pattern type, get pattern_id from the database;
  Rules[new_rule_id].pattern_type = pattern_id;
  Define Rules[new_rule_id].case_action;
  Save the cornerstone case (JSON) in
      Rules[new_rule_id].cornerstone_case;
  IF trigger_rule_id < rule_size
    IF trigger_inf == 'true' THEN
      Rules[new_rule_id].inf_action_true
          = Rules[trigger_rule_id].inf_action_true;
      Rules[new_rule_id].inf_action_false
          = Rules[trigger_rule_id].inf_action_true;
      Rules[trigger_rule_id].inf_action_true = new_rule_id;
    ELSE IF trigger_inf == 'false' THEN
      Rules[new_rule_id].inf_action_true
          = Rules[trigger_rule_id].inf_action_false;
      Rules[new_rule_id].inf_action_false
          = Rules[trigger_rule_id].inf_action_false;
      Rules[trigger_rule_id].inf_action_false = new_rule_id;
    END IF
  ELSE
    Rules[new_rule_id].inf_action_true = -1;
    Rules[new_rule_id].inf_action_false = -1;
    IF trigger_inf == 'true' THEN
      Rules[trigger_rule_id].inf_action_true = new_rule_id;
    ELSE IF trigger_inf == 'false' THEN
      Rules[trigger_rule_id].inf_action_false = new_rule_id;
    END IF
  END IF
END
```

Fig. 4. The algorithm of rule addition.

In order to ensure all pre-processing can be repeated by finance researchers even after rule addition, the platform needs to keep the set of inference actions at any stage of rule evolution. Therefore, an important feature is introduced: before adding any new rule, the old inference actions are copied and stored along with the rule. If finance researchers would later repeat whatever they have done using old rule sets at any point of the rule base evolution, they are able to select previous rule sets by simply selecting the right rule size. For instance, if the user selects to run the rule set that has a size of 5, the system will use the set of inference actions saved for the rule set of that particular size (i.e. the rule set when the size was 5).

The updated algorithm to add a new rule is shown in Fig. 4, which reflects all the new features of the system.

4 Case Study

In the case study, we will run three different tools to pre-process Sirca [20] daily stock data in two different scenarios:

4.1 Scenario 1 - Eliminating Duplicate Dividends

Financial studies such as event studies often require the computation of a company returns over a period of time. However, the value of these returns is affected by corporate actions such as the issuing of dividends. A dividend denotes a payment made by a firm out of its current or accumulated retained earnings to its owners, which gives rise to a fall of the stock price by the dividend amount on the executive date. Although the information on corporate actions is available in the data, processing it is a non-trivial task due to the need to deal with duplicate dividend announcement records. There are totally six cases that result in an incremental modification of the rules (business logic). Table 1 illustrates different cases for handling this problem.

Specifically, in the most common cases, like Case 1 shown in Table 1(a), duplicate events are considered simply as two dividend events with the same timestamp, the same Div Amt. and the same Div Ex Date. Later, in the new case (Case 2) shown in Table 1(b), the Div Ex Date in this Dividend event refers to a day that has no trading, which means this Dividend event may not be valid. This needs to be reported in the output so the financial researcher can avoid the potential errors caused. Thus, a new rule should be defined to rectify the issue. Similarly, other new cases all result in changes of the existing rules.

In this scenario, using our new method (incremental rule management), we initially defined 3 rules (Table 2(a)), and then after 4 iterations, we finally got 7 rules (Table 2 (b)). Table 2(c) displays all the event pattern types used in this eliminating duplicate dividends scenario.

4.2 Scenario 2 - Earnings Annualisation

This is a more complicated scenario, which can better show the capability of the new system in handling rules involving time handling (in other words complex event processing). In some financial studies, researchers need to calculate and compare the Price-Earnings ratios (P/E) of different companies in the same industry to indicate whether investors of a particular company are expecting higher earnings growth in the future than other companies. This is a very important measure for investors to assess a company. P/E equals market value per share (i.e. price) divided by earnings per share.

P/E = Price/Earnings per share

Thus, to calculate P/E ratio, we need both price data that provides price information and corporate action data that provides earnings information.

Table 1. Different cases in eliminating duplicate dividends

(a) Case 1 – Simple duplicate dividend records: two events with Type "Dividend" has the same timestamp, the same "Div Amt." and the same "Div Ex Date".

#RIC	Date	Type	Div Ex Date	Div Amt	Div ID	Div Delete Marker	Payment Status
ABC	12/08/2012	Dividend	11/09/2012	0.07	7885540	0	APPD
ABC	12/08/2012	Dividend	11/09/2012	0.07	7885540	0	APPD

(b) Case 2 – No "End Of Day" event exists with "Div Ex Date" of a "Dividend" event as the timestamp.

#RIC	Date	Type	Div Ex Date	Div Amt	Div ID	Div Delete Marker	Payment Status
ABC	12/08/2012	Dividend	*11/09/2012*	0.07	7885540	0	APPD

(c) Case 3 – An event with the type "Dividend" has null or empty value in the field "Div Amt." or "Div Ex Date".

#RIC	Date	Type	Div Ex Date	Div Amt	Div ID	Div Delete Marker	Payment Status
ABC	15/10/2013	Dividend			9344378	0	APPD

(d) Case 4 – Although these two dividends are issued at the same time (Date), the Div IDs are different which indicates they are two different dividends rather than a duplicate.

#RIC	Date	Type	Div Ex Date	Div Amt	Div ID	Div Delete Marker	Payment Status
ABC	12/08/2012	Dividend	11/09/2012	0.07	7885540	0	APPD
ABC	12/08/2012	Dividend	11/10/2012	0.07	7926058	0	APPD

(e) Case 5 – A "Dividend" event has a value other than "APPD" in the field "Payment Status". This dividend event is not approved (a value other than APPD) so it should be considered as an out-dated record.

#RIC	Date	Type	Div Ex Date	Div Amt	Div ID	Div Delete Marker	Payment Status
ABC	12/08/2012	Dividend	11/09/2012	0.08	7885540	0	PROP

(f) Case 6 – A "Dividend" event has '1' in the field "Div Delete Marker". This dividend event is virtually deleted by the data provider, so this is not a valid entry.

#RIC	Date	Type	Div Ex Date	Div Amt	Div ID	Div Delete Marker	Payment Status
ABC	26/08/2014	Dividend	11/09/2012	0.15	9654412	1	APPD

The task here is to find the correct value of earnings per share from Earning data for each trading day (End Of Day event) in TRTH data. There are totally six cases we have incrementally found that result in an incremental modification on the rules (business logic). The cases are displayed in Table 3.

At the first stage, the financial researcher defined a rule based on the most common cases like Case 1 shown in Table 3(a). The content of the rule is:

Table 2. Initial and final rules for eliminating duplicate dividends

(a) Initial rule set for eliminating duplicate dividends

Rule No.	Event pattern type	Action	Inf. action (true)	Inf. action (false)
1	Dividend event	N/A	2	2
2	Duplicate Dividends	Delete the former one	3	3
3	Missing an EOD event on DED	Report it as an error	-1	-1

(b) Final rule set for eliminating duplicate dividends

Rule No.	Event pattern type	Action	Inf. action (true)	Inf. action (false)
1	Dividend event	N/A	*4*	2
2	Duplicate Dividends	Delete the former one	*5*	3
3	Missing an EOD event on DED	Report it as an error	-1	-1
4	Missing value in a Div event	***Discard this Div event and report missing value***	*2*	*2*
5	Different Div ID	***Retrieve the last action***	*3*	*6*
6	Status is not 'APPD'	***Retrieve the last action***	*3*	*7*
7	Delete Marker is not 0	***Retrieve the last action***	*3*	*3*

(c) Specifications of event pattern types for eliminating duplicate dividends

ID	Name	Event Pattern Description
1	Dividend event	An event is a "Dividend" event.
2	Duplicate Dividends	Two events with Type "Dividend" have the same timestamp, the same "Div Amt." and the same "Div Ex Date".
3	Missing an EOD event on DED	No "End Of Day" event exists with "Div Ex Date" of a "Dividend" event as the timestamp.
4	Missing value in a Div event	An event with the type "Dividend" has null or empty value in the field "Div Amt." or "Div Ex Date".
5	Different Div ID	A pair of duplicate dividends (pattern type No. 4) have different "Div Mkt Lvl ID".
6	Status is not 'APPD'	A "Dividend" event has a value other than 'APPD' in the field "Payment Status".
7	Delete Marker is not '0'	A "Dividend" event has '1' in the field "Div Delete Marker".

If an event with type "Earning""(E) happens before an event with type "End Of Day" (EOD) (Note that for each EOD find only one closest occurrence if it exists),
then *the "earnings per share" or this EOD event should be calculated by* $E.epsAmount * 10^{EPS\_scaling\_factor}$ [1].

---

[1] "epsAmount" denotes the value of the field "EPS Amount" in the "Earning" event, and "EPS_scaling_factor" denotes the value of the field "EPS Scaling Factor".

Table 3. Different cases considered in calculating earnings.

(a) Case 1 – Normal earning record.

RIC	Date	Type	EPS Period End Date	EPS Period Length	EPS Amount	EPS Scaling Factor
ABC	17/08/2011	Earning	30/06/2011	12	2306.9	-4
ABC	18/08/2011	EndOfDay				

(b) Case 2 – 6 months' earnings + 6 months' earnings.

RIC	Date	Type	EPS Period End Date	EPS Period Length	EPS Amount	EPS Scaling Factor
ABC	28/02/2012	Earning	31/12/2011	6	2071.7	-4
ABC	22/08/2012	Earning	30/06/2012	6	7974	-5
ABC	23/08/2012	EndOfDay				

(c) Case 3 – 3 months' earnings + 3 months' earnings + 6 months' earnings.

RIC	Date	Type	EPS Period End Date	EPS Period Length	EPS Amount	EPS Scaling Factor
ABC	28/02/2011	Earning	31/12/2011	3	952.5	-4
ABC	25/05/2012	Earning	31/03/2012	3	1350.6	-4
ABC	22/08/2012	Earning	30/06/2012	6	2011.3	-4
ABC	23/08/2012	EndOfDay				

(d) Case 4 – 3 months' earnings + 9 months' earnings.

RIC	Date	Type	EPS Period End Date	EPS Period Length	EPS Amount	EPS Scaling Factor
ABC	28/02/2012	Earning	31/12/2011	3	874	-4
ABC	25/05/2012	Earning	31/03/2012	9	1985	-4
ABC	26/05/2012	EndOfDay				

(e) Case 5 – 3 months' earnings + 3 months' earnings
+ 3 months' earnings + 3 months' earnings.

RIC	Date	Type	EPS Period End Date	EPS Period Length	EPS Amount	EPS Scaling Factor
ABC	28/02/2011	Earning	30/9/2011	3	522	-4
ABC	25/05/2012	Earning	31/12/2011	3	887	-4
ABC	22/08/2012	Earning	31/03/2012	3	1397.3	-4
ABC	22/08/2012	Earning	30/06/2012	3	4352	-5
ABC	26/05/2012	EndOfDay				

(f) Case 6 – 9 months' earnings + 3 months' earnings.

RIC	Date	Type	EPS Period End Date	EPS Period Length	EPS Amount	EPS Scaling Factor
ABC	28/02/2012	Earning	31/12/2011	9	2004	-4
ABC	28/02/2013	Earning	30/09/2012	3	1085.4	-4
ABC	01/03/2013	EndOfDay				

After a while, the financial researcher found some new cases like the one (Case 2) shown in Table 3(b) that caused incorrect calculation using the previous rule. In this case, there are Earning events with 6 (months) as the value of the EPS Period Length field rather than 12 (month) as in the most common cases. The financial researcher decided to annualise the Earning events, i.e. find two Earning events with 6 month EPS Period Length and add up EPS Amount values in these two records so their EPS periods together constitute one year. Thus, the calculation of the earnings of the End Of Day event should be changed. Similarly, other new cases all result in changes of the existing rules.

In this scenario, using our new method (incremental rule management), we initially defined only one rule (Table 4(a)), and then after 5 iterations, we finally got 6 rules (Table 4(b)). In Table 4, E denotes an earnings record, and EOD denotes an End-of-day record (price data). An arrow defines the chronological order of two records.

Table 4. Initial and final rules for earnings annualisation

(a) Initial rule set for earnings annualisation

Rule No.	Event pattern type	Action	Inf. action (true)	Inf. action (false)
1	Earning before End Of Day	$EOD.earnings = E.epsAmount * 10^{EPS\_scaling\_factor}$	-1	-1

(b) Final rule set for earnings annualisation

Rule No.	Event pattern type	Action	Inf. action (true)	Inf. action (false)
1	Earning before End Of Day	$EOD.earnings = E.epsAmount * 10^{EPS\_scaling\_factor}$	2	2
2	Two 6-month earnings before End Of Day	$EOD.earnings = (E_{6(1)}.epsAmount + E_{6(2)}.epsAmount) * 10^{EPS\_scaling\_factor}$	3	3
3	Two 3-month earnings and one 6-month earning before End Of Day	$EOD.earnings = (E_{6}.epsAmount + E_{3(1)}.epsAmount + E_{3(2)}.epsAmount) * 10^{EPS\_scaling\_factor}$	4	4
4	One 3-month earning and one 9-month earning before End Of Day	$EOD.earnings = E_{9}.epsAmount + E_{3}.epsAmount$	5	5
5	Four 3-month earnings before End Of Day	$EOD.earnings = (E_{3(1)}.epsAmount + E_{3(2)}.epsAmount + E_{3(3)}.epsAmount + E_{3(4)}.epsAmount) * 10^{EPS\_scaling\_factor}$	6	6
6	One 9-month earning and one 3-month earning before End Of Day	$EOD.earnings = (E_{3}.epsAmount + E_{9}.epsAmount) * 10^{EPS\_scaling\_factor}$	-1	-1

(Continued)

Table 4. (*Continued*)

(c) Specifications of the event pattern types for earnings annualisation

ID	Name	Event Pattern Description
1	Earning before End Of Day	$E \to EOD$ An event with type "Earning" (E) happens before an event with type "End Of Day" (EOD). (Find only one closest occurrence for each EOD if it exists.)
2	Two 6-month earnings before End Of Day	$E_{6(2)} \to E_{6(1)} \to EOD$ Two events $E_{6(1)}$ and $E_{6(2)}$ with type "Earning" ($E_{6(2)}$ before $E_{6(1)}$) happen before an event with type "End Of Day" (EOD) with: • The "EPS Period Length" of both $E_{6(1)}$ and $E_{6(2)}$ is 6; • $E_{6(2)}.epsEndDate + E_{6(2)}.epsLength = E_{6(1)}.epsEndDate$ • Find only one closest occurrence for each EOD if it exists.
3	Two 3-month earnings and one 6-month earning before End Of Day	$E_{3(2)} \to E_{3(1)} \to E_6 \to EOD$ Three events with type "Earning" ($E_{3(2)}$ before $E_{3(1)}$ before E_6) happen before an event with type "End Of Day" (EOD) with: • The "EPS Period Length" of $E_{3(2)}$ and $E_{3(1)}$ is 3; The "EPS Period Length" of E_6 is 6; • $E_{3(2)}.epsEndDate + E_{3(2)}.epsLength = E_{3(1)}.epsEndDate$ • $E_{3(1)}.epsEndDate + E_{3(1)}.epsLength = E_6.epsEndDate$ • Find only one closest occurrence for each EOD if it exists.
4	One 3-month earning and one 9-month earning before End Of Day	$E_3 \to E_9 \to EOD$ Two events E_3 and E_9 with type "Earning" (E_3 before E_9) happen before an event with type "End Of Day" (EOD) with: • The "EPS Period Length" of E_3 is 3 and The "EPS Period Length" of E_9 is 9; • $E_3.epsEndDate + E_3.epsLength = E_9.epsEndDate$ • Find only one closest occurrence for each EOD if it exists.
5	Four 3-month earnings before End Of Day	$E_{3(4)} \to E_{3(3)} \to E_{3(2)} \to E_{3(1)} \to EOD$ Four events $E_{3(1)}$, $E_{3(2)}$, $E_{3(3)}$, and $E_{3(4)}$ with type "Earning" ($E_{3(4)}$ before $E_{3(3)}$ before $E_{3(2)}$ before $E_{3(1)}$) happen before an event with type "End Of Day" (EOD) with: • The "EPS Period Length" of $E_{3(1)}$, $E_{3(2)}$, $E_{3(3)}$, and $E_{3(4)}$ is 3; • $E_{3(i)}.epsEndDate + E_{3(i)}.epsLength = E_{3(i-1)}.epsEndDate$ (i=2,3,4) • Find only one closest occurrence for each EOD if it exists.
6	One 9-month earning and one 3-month earning before End Of Day	$E_9 \to E_3 \to EOD$ Two events E_3 and E_9 with type "Earning" (E_9 before E_3) happen before an event with type "End Of Day" (EOD) with: • The "EPS Period Length" of E_3 is 3 and The "EPS Period Length" of E_9 is 9; • $E_9.epsEndDate + E_9.epsLength = E_3.epsEndDate$ • Find only one closest occurrence for each EOD if it exists.

Table 4(c) displays all the event pattern types used in this earnings annualisation scenario. In this table, an arrow defines the chronological order of two events, i.e. a -> b means a happens strictly before b (we do not count it when a and b happen on the same date); E_n means an Earning event with n as the value of EPS Period Length; EOD denotes an End-of-day event (price data); epsEndDate denotes the field EPS Period End Date; epsLength denotes the field EPS Period Length.

4.3   Prototype Implementation and Tests

We modified the previous prototype of the proposed EP-RDR architecture in Java to reflect the updates on the design with a graphical user interface which allows users to define RDR rules as well as simple event pattern types. The underlying rule processor is a Java program that implements the rule processing logic. All event pattern definitions/code and rules are stored in PostgreSQL relational databases. The EPDaaS component can invoke two different EPSs. The first one is a simple EPS for initial validation [17]; the second one is a powerful commercial EPS called EventSwarm developed by Deontik [14], which has proven successful in real-time analytics for data streams in the health domain [21]. Once the RDR component sends the request to the EPDaaS, either EventSwarm or the simple EPS (EventSwarm has the higher priority) start to detect occurrences of the specific event pattern type. The output of detected event pattern occurrences are in JSON format, and saved in a stack repository.

Table 5. Other tools used in the experiments to be compared with EP-RDR.

Abbr.	Name	Description
BP	Bespoke Program	A dedicated program that implements the data pre-processing logic in Java for both the "eliminating duplicate dividends" scenario and the "calculating earnings" scenario.
OP	OpenRefine	One of the most popular and free desktop applications for data pre-processing, previously funded by Google. This tool is easy to use but data pre-processing business logic is performed manually by financial researchers.

In real life scenarios, financial researchers either employ a programmer to develop a bespoke program, or learn and apply an existing data pre-processing tool to perform pre-processing tasks on datasets. Therefore, we have selected two tools to be compared with our new system (EP-RDR) in the experiments (see Table 5). One of them is a bespoke program (BP) we developed which implements the data pre-processing logic in Java for both the eliminating duplicate dividends scenario and the earnings annualisation scenario. The other one is OpenRefine (OP), which is a popular and representative data pre-processing tool that is broadly utilised in various domains. Note that we have excluded existing EPSs in the experiments as they require too much IT expertise.

The three tools to be compared include the updated EP-RDR prototype (EP-RDR), a bespoke program (BP) we developed with the data pre-processing logic for both scenarios implemented, and OpenRefine (OR). The reason why we select these tools is that each of them represent a type of existing solution for financial data pre-processing and none of them require any IT expertise to get it to work.

5   Experimental Results

5.1   Automation, Customisation and Time-Handling Assessment

In the scenario of dividend duplicate detection, we tried to build the final rule set in the three tools - BP, OR and EP-RDR respectively. BP required an IT expert to implement the rules and it took several days for each rule to be implemented. In OR, not all the rules can be implemented, e.g. time-related rules (Rule 3 in Table 2(b)). In EP-RDR, the rule building process was much easier, and took only 5 min for each rule to be added. We also asked a financial expert with very limited IT knowledge to try customising the system with these rules and it was successfully done within an hour without assistance by any IT expert. Then we executed the defined rule set on 22 Australian companies to see if the pre-processing can be completed automatically by the three tools. OR can automate merely those successfully defined rules though it requires exporting them into a JSON file first and then apply them to each of the companies. BP and EP-RDR can finish all these rules automatically.

In the scenario of earnings annualisation, OR was completely not capable as all the rules requires time handling (i.e. event pattern detection). BP and EP-RDR could handle these time-related rules and automate the process but BP must be implemented by an IT expert and EP-RDR could be customised by financial experts.

5.2   Evolution Assessment

We conducted an experiment in the eliminating duplicate dividends scenario to compare the rule change efficiency of both BP, OP and EP-RDR. Specifically, we ran the initial rule set (see Table 2(a)) on twenty-two Australian companies to detect duplicate dividends and calculate returns, and then used the results to conduct an event study on the dividend effective date respectively. Once we found the event study result is not reasonable, we then tried to make changes to the rule base according to Case 3 in Table 1(c). And finally we calculated the rule change efficiency (RCE) of each system using this formula:

$$RCE = (1 - \% \text{ of duplicate dividends not removed}) / \text{No. of rules changed}$$

In this case, we know that there should be totally 300 dividends removed due to duplicate dividends or invalid entries (missing values).

Specifically, the initial rule set used as the pre-processing logic in all systems is the three rules shown in Table 2(a). We executed the three rules in both BP and EP-RDR and conduct event studies using the output results. We found unreasonable event study results due to missing values in dividend data. Thus, we modified the code of BP; and we added a new rule in the rule set used by EP-RDR (Rule 4 in Table 2(b)). We found that in regard to BP, changes on one particular rule normally affect some other rules. The change of the first rule in the initial rule set affected the two other following rules, which resulted in three iterations of changes and therefore three repetitions of the same event studies. In fact, it took quite a long time to have it work in the right way. In OP, it is the same case as BP but for Rule 3 (a time-related rule) cannot be well-defined. By contrast, in EP-RDR, we just added one rule (Rule 4 in Table 2(b)) and the existing rules are not affected, so the result came out correctly, thereby eliminating the hassle of repeating event studies. Table 4 shows the comparison of rule change efficiency of the three systems.

Compared with BP and OP, EP-RDR enables the financial researcher to update the rule base simply and neatly without assistance from the IT expert, consuming a significantly less amount of time. Therefore, we can draw a conclusion that the efficiency of rule changes in our new system out-performs BP and OP (Table 6).

Table 6. Comparison in rule change efficiency.

Tool	Rules changed	Total duplicates not removed	Event study repetitions	Rule Change Efficiency (RCE)
BP & OP	1	300/300	3	33.3%
	2	12/100		
	3	0/100		
EP-RDR	1	0/300	1	100%

5.3 Repeatability Assessment

In both scenarios, in BP, once the program is modified, it cannot be converted back so previous rules at earlier stages cannot be repeated; in OP, we need to save the rule set manually in a JSON file at any stage for future use; otherwise, the rules will not be retained; in EP-RDR, we were able to execute previous rule sets at any stage of the rule evolution process.

5.4   Discussion

A bespoke program is normally dedicated to automating a specific data pre-processing logic, which can hardly be customised by users. Time-related issues might be specifically handled but normally it is very inefficient.

Data pre-processing tools are primarily designed for one-off manual tasks. Users can customise the tool to their own needs by applying faceting, clustering, etc. to their datasets step by step (i.e. it is not fully automatic). Although some data pre-processing tools like OpenRefine provides the function to save all used rules as a JSON file so users can apply it to similar datasets automatically, this is still extremely error-prone. Most importantly, data pre-cessing tools like OpenRefine are not capable in addressing time-related issues. These issues can be handled well by EPSs but they require too much IT expertise to be customised and managed.

Neither BP nor OP satisfies the last two criteria of *ACTER*. Specifically, using these two tools, financial researchers can hardly evolve the system without IT experts assistance; financial market data pre-processing cannot be repeated when there has been any change on the system (e.g. the rule base).

On the contrary, the new EP-RDR system proves to have met all the *ACTER* criteria. Specifically:

- Automation (A) – Any set of rules built through the system can be executed in one go automatically;
- Customisation (C) – Finance researchers can customise the system according to their own needs by building their own rule base;
- Time handling (T) – EPDaaS as a component plays the role of detecting event pattern occurrences, so the system can handle time- related issues effectively;
- Evolution (E) – With the involvement of RDR, the system allows for incremental, error-triggered rule management, i.e. adding a new rule when an incorrect action is inspected without corrupting the existing rule base;

Table 7. How do existing potential solutions meet the criteria ($\sqrt{}$: Yes, ×: No, $\sqrt{}$*: Possibly yes but not efficient)

Tools	A	C	T	E	R
Bespoke software	$\sqrt{}$	×	$\sqrt{}$*	×	×
Data pre-processing tools	$\sqrt{}$*	$\sqrt{}$	×	×	$\sqrt{}$*
Event processing systems	$\sqrt{}$*	×	$\sqrt{}$	×	×
EP-RDR prototype	$\sqrt{}$	$\sqrt{}$	$\sqrt{}$	$\sqrt{}$	$\sqrt{}$

- Repeatability (R) – With all inference actions always kept along with existing rules at any stage of the rule base evolution, finance researchers can run historical rule sets so as to repeat whatever has been done before.

Table 5 summarises how successful these tools are to meet the ACTER criteria (Table 7).

6 Conclusion

In this paper, we have discussed the significance of financial market data pre-processing for financial studies and the current challenges. We have also suggested 5 criteria to assess financial market data pre-processing tools, including automatability, customisability, time-handleability, evolvability and repeatability (*ACTER*), with an emphasis on the last three criteria, which are often not well handled by existing tools. We have updated and extended our previous work - an architecture called EP-RDR for building and maintaining user-driven data analysis, in which a Ripple-Down Rule (RDR) framework is integrated with an event pattern detection service. Some new features are introduced so as to satisfy all the *ACTER* criteria.

We then applied the *ACTER* criteria on EP-RDR as well as some other existing tools in the context of two real-life pre-processing scenarios in a financial study (eliminating duplicate dividends and earnings annualisation) to compare the desirability of these tools for financial market data pre-processing. EP-RDR proves to have outperformed other tools in terms of the suitability to conduct financial market data pre-processing tasks by satisfying all the criteria.

References

1. Han, J., Kamber, M.: Data Mining: Concepts and Techniques, 2nd edn. Morgan Kaufmann Publishers, San Francisco, CA, USA (2006)
2. Binder, J.: The event study methodology since 1969. In: Review of Quantitative Finance and Accounting, vol. 11, pp. 111–137 1998/09/01 1998
3. Eventus. (2012). http://www.eventstudy.com/
4. Compton, P., Jansen, R.: Knowledge in context: a strategy for expert system maintenance. In: 2nd Australian Joint Artificial Intelligence Conference, pp. 292–306 (1988)
5. Bitterer, A.: Who's Who in Open-Source Data Quality, 18 January 2012
6. IBM. (2009). IBM Quality Stage. http://www-01.ibm.com/software/data/infosphere/qualitystage/
7. SAP (2011). Data Quality Management. www.sap.com
8. Friedman, T., Bitterer, A.: Magic Quadrant for Data Quality Tools, 28 July 2011
9. OpenRefine. (2015). http://openrefine.org/
10. Etzion, O., Niblett, P.: Event Processing in Action. Manning Publications Co, Greenwich (2011)
11. Esper (2013). http://esper.codehaus.org/
12. RedHat (2015). Drools Fusion. http://drools.jboss.org/drools-fusion.html
13. SoftwareAG (2015). Apama. http://www.softwareag.com/corporate/products/apama_webmethods/analytics/overview/default.asp
14. Deontik (2013). EventSwarm. http://deontik.com/Products/EventSwarm.html
15. Luckham, D.: (2006). What's the Difference Between ESP and CEP? http://www.complexevents.com/?p=103
16. Hinze, A., Sachs, K., Buchmann, A.: Event-based applications and enabling technologies. In: Presented at the Proceedings of the Third ACM International Conference on Distributed Event-Based Systems, Nashville, Tennessee (2009)

17. Chen, W., Rabhi, F.: An RDR-based approach for event data analysis. In: Presented at the Third Australasian Symposium on Service Research and Innovation (ASSRI 2013), Sydney, Australia (2013)
18. Richards, D.: Two decades of ripple down rules research. Knowl. Eng. Rev. **24**(2), 159–184 (2009)
19. Compton, P., Peters, L., Edwards, G., Lavers, T.G.: Experience with Ripple-Down Rules. Knowl. Based Syst. **19**, 356–362 (2006)
20. Sirca (2015). http://www.sirca.org.au/
21. Berry, A., Milosevic, Z.: Real-time analytics for legacy data streams in health: monitoring health data quality. In: Presented at the 17th IEEE International Enterprise Distributed Object Computing Conference (EDOC), 2013, Vancouver, BC (2013)

Strategic Competitive Advantages Through Enterprise Systems: The Case of Exchange Systems

Martin Haferkorn[✉], Michael Siering, and Kai Zimmermann

Goethe University Frankfurt, Grüneburgplatz 1,
60323 Frankfurt am Main, Germany
{haferkorn, siering, kzimmermann}@wiwi.uni-frankfurt.de

Abstract. Enterprise Systems play a key role in securities trading. Exchange operators spend great effort in overhauling their IT-infrastructure to satisfy the needs of market participants who require faster and more resilient order management cycles. Previous studies have disregarded the question whether such specific IT-investments lead to competitive advantages. Against this background, we empirically analyze the impact of exchange system upgrades on the market share of the respective exchange. Using a benchmarking approach against the closest competitor, we find that exchange system overhauls significantly increase the attracted trading volume. We conclude that investments in enterprise systems provide benefits and lead to competitive advantages for the upgrading firm.

Keywords: Strategic IT advantage · Enterprise systems · Exchange systems · Execution speed

1 Introduction

Enterprise systems play a key role in many firms since they are applied to integrate the data used within an organization and help to manage and allocate a firm's resources and processes [1]. Thus, a large body of literature has recognized the important role of enterprise systems and the consequences of IT-investments on corporate performance [1]. However, many studies focus on the long-term impact of such investments and neglect that due to increased competition, strategic advantages may decrease over time which makes it hard to measure the impact of the introduction of new technologies.

Especially in the financial domain, information systems play an important role in the firms' business processes. For instance, exchange operators use information systems to manage their key process: i.e. handling and matching the customers' orders. Since the advent of high-frequency trading (HFT), market participants apply strategies where orders are submitted, canceled and executed within very short periods of time. Therefore, the speed of managing the order life cycle can represent a strategic advantage for exchange operators if they are able to handle and match orders faster than other competitors. Consequently, the financial services industry is very suitable to measure the impact of single IT-investments since the consequences of these

© Springer International Publishing Switzerland 2015
A. Lugmayr (Ed.): FinanceCom 2014, LNBIP 217, pp. 79–89, 2015.
DOI: 10.1007/978-3-319-28151-3_6

IT-innovations can be quantified easily. This is especially the case for exchanges as the competitive position can be calculated on a daily basis by comparing the end of day volume.

In previous research, different studies have already analyzed the effects of investments in exchange systems on market quality. For instance, it has been found that spreads decrease after latency reducing IT-updates, thus market quality increases [2]. However, the introduction of new exchange systems is often accompanied by changes of the market model, which makes it hard to attribute the measured effects to the respective infrastructure investments only [3]. Overall, previous studies focus at the market level, i.e. measuring the change in market quality parameters like spread or volatility following these exchange system updates. However, these studies do not consider whether exchange operators gain a competitive advantage from the introduction of new exchange systems.

With our study, we close this research gap by empirically examining whether IT-investments in exchange systems, which are the main enterprise systems for exchanges, lead to a competitive advantage for their operators. Therefore, we take into account recent IT-updates of two European exchanges. We benchmark the trading volume and therefore the revenue potential for the major stock indices traded on these exchanges against their most important competitor to investigate whether exchange operators can establish a competitive advantage. Thus, we contribute to the research stream on competitive advantages of information systems in general and exchange systems in particular.

The remainder of this paper is structured as follows. In Sect. 2, we present the research background of our study, encompassing the research stream on strategic advantages through enterprise systems introduction and usage followed by literature on enterprise systems in securities markets. In Sect. 3, we present our research methodology whereas the results of our empirical study are outlined in Sect. 4. Finally, Sect. 5 concludes.

2 Research Background

2.1 Strategic Advantages Through Enterprise Systems Usage

Enterprise systems encompass information systems enabling a company to "integrate the data used throughout its entire organization" [1] and thus help organizations to manage their key resources and processes. In this context, a large body of literature has already theoretically and empirically analyzed which benefits and strategic advantages arise from information systems usage in general and from enterprise system usage in particular [4]. In this context, enterprise systems are seen as a part of a firm's IT-infrastructure which, in combination with human IT-resources and intangible IT-enabled resources, forms the IT-based resources of a firm [4]. In this regard, it is of utter importance for the sustainability of a comparative advantage resulting from IT-based resources that next to the IT-based resources' value for the firm, these are also heterogeneously distributed across competitors [5]. In general, these advantages are sustainable if the IT-based resources are imperfectly mobile, otherwise, competitors can also invest in the same resources and the comparative advantage is only temporary [5].

Consequently, the impact of using and investing in IT-based resources has been of interest in a number of studies which typically relate a measure for IT to a performance measure [6, 7]. For instance, the yearly budget spent for IT may be related to the net income per employee [6, 8]. Thus, different studies find a positive impact of IT on revenue growth [6] or employee productivity [8]. However, another stream of research reports that despite from increasing IT-investments overall productivity growth has stagnated [9]. This may be caused by measurement errors (for instance caused by different accounting principles or different accounting options taken by firms) or by the fact that the payoffs of IT might take some time until they are fully realized. Finally, and most importantly, possible comparative advantages through IT-investments made by one company may be canceled out by other investments [10].

Quantifying the comparative advantage caused by single IT-investments is hard to measure due to several problems. For instance, several approaches rely on data based on balance sheets. As balance sheet figures are published periodically (e.g. quarterly or yearly), financial performance metrics cannot be attributed to single IT-investments since other factors, i.e. innovations or actions of competitors, influence firm key performance indicators as well. Consequently, previous research has only focused on general measures like IT-innovativeness or IT-budget which were analyzed for comparatively long time periods [4]. In contrast, in case of industries especially relying on IT-intensive business processes, single IT-investments can have a tremendous impact on firm performance and strategic positioning, which requires a precise measurement of the consequent effects. This is especially the case in the financial services industry.

2.2 Enterprise Systems in Securities Markets

Exchange operators in securities markets represent a group of firms whose success heavily depends on their IT-based resources managing the main business process, i.e. providing market participants with the opportunity to buy or sell securities. Due to increasing competition among exchange operators, the sustainability of advantages caused by IT-investments is reduced as competitors are also able to invest in new IT-systems. This circumstance requires a more precise and timely measurement. As of 2014, trading activities mostly rely on electronic order books, where resulting prices are determined by electronic order matchers. As the amount of information in a globally connected economy increases, the speed of the provided infrastructure has gained increased importance.

The importance of these exchange systems is further intensified in face of recent technical developments, i.e. the emergence of high frequency trading which focuses on submitting an increased number of orders in short periods of time. In the U.S., HFT-based trading has a market share of 61 % (in 2009) [11] and 77 % in the UK (in 2011) [12]. Since the amount of traders employing HFT still increases, exchanges have to adjust their systems to satisfy these customers who demand reliable and, most important, fast exchange systems. Thus, exchange operators are competing in terms of execution speed resulting in a major overhaul of legacy exchange systems all over the world, which raises the question whether these large IT-investments can be justified from an economic standpoint.

Despite facing these difficulties for exchange operators, research in the field of exchange system overhauls is still scarce. Previous studies mostly focus on the question of whether these overhauls improve market conditions by measuring a stock market's quality, for instance by taking into account effects on market liquidity. A fundamental study in this field is conducted by [3] who analyze the effects of the introduction of a hybrid market model along with an exchange system upgrade at the NYSE. They find that implicit trading costs (measured by means of the spread) rise while the variability of prices (volatility) decreases. However, they are not able to solely attribute these effects to a software-upgrade, since the applied market model affecting these parameters was altered as well.

Taking an IT-overhaul at Deutsche Boerse into account, [2] analyze the impact of new technology reducing latency from 50 ms to 10 ms, representing an increase in order update speed. They show that this upgrade was beneficial for small- and medium-sized stocks in terms of decreasing spreads. However, they do not analyze the changes in the number of trades and thus no effect on the exchange operator's profits could be shown. With the same focus on execution speed, [13] study the effects of an IT-upgrade on trading volume and spread at the Tokyo Stock Exchange. They conclude that spread and trade size decline, accompanied by an increase in execution frequency and number of trades carried out. The same event is studied by [14], observing the same effects and additionally showing that volatility decreases and liquidity increases. Especially the increase of the number of trades by 6 % at the Tokyo Stock Exchange has a positive effect on the exchange operator's revenue stream, as exchanges earn money by the volume traded on their platform. As the overhaul of such a crucial enterprise system is costly and connected with several risks, it is of great interest whether IT-investments lead to a strategic advantage for the investing exchange operator. With this paper, we aim at answering this fundamental question.

2.3 Recent Exchange Systems Overhauls

Since the customers' requirements for lower latency could not be appropriately met by legacy systems employed at most exchanges, market operators are in need to overhaul their systems to keep up with these customer's requirements. Within this study, we select two cases of IT overhauls in 2012 focusing on speed improvements and thus aiming at reaching competitive advantages in comparison to the exchanges' competitors. As we want to observe the effect of the exchange trading system update solely, we also ensure that no meaningful changes in the market model were made along with the introduction of the new system. We consider overhauls at two exchanges, i.e. Oslo Børs (OB) and SIX Swiss Exchange (SIX), both operating within Europe. Thereby, we avoid influences caused by different market system requirements and potential side effects by varying regulatory frameworks as we focus on European exchanges solely.

On April 23rd, 2012, SIX announced the introduction of the SWXess-exchange system, which was developed by NASDAQ OMX and is based on X-stream INET. Appraising the exchange system as one of the most modern exchange systems in terms of capacity and latency, the latency is supposed to be reduced from 800 ms to 37 ms. Furthermore, due to the importance of low latency trading, SIX also claim a new competitive position as they operated the fastest exchange system in Europe at the time of introduction. In addition to the cut in latency, SIX introduced co-location services, a service where market participants are allowed to place their trading systems directly within the exchange's data center [15].

The new exchange system at OB was launched on November 12th, 2012. Like the exchange system of SIX, it is based on a platform which was used on a different exchange before, i.e. the Millennium Exchange trading platform. The Millennium Exchange trading platform was developed by the London Stock Exchange (LSE) and is operated at LSE since February 2011. The exchange system was introduced and customized by the developing company MillenniumIT and LSE, like SIX, OB used external expertise of the developing company to customize their system. Comparable to the exchange system overhaul by SIX as well as to other exchange system overhauls, the new system decreases the latency of OB significantly [16].

Both exchange systems were updated in 2012, at a time where competition in European securities trading was intensified through the implementation of the European Markets in Financial Instruments Directive (MiFID) regulation [17]. Since its application, new trading venues, called multilateral trading facilities (MTF), were enabled to compete with established exchanges (Regulated Markets (RM)) by offering substitutive stock trading opportunities. In 2012, MTF could claim market shares in multiple European stock indices, which enables a direct comparison of trading volume changes in relation to competitors after exchange infrastructure investments [18].

3 Research Methodology and Dataset Description

3.1 Methodological Considerations

In order to examine whether IT-investments can actually tip the balance within the European competition for order flow and provide impact on firm performance and strategic positioning, we apply an event-based regression analysis on the two latest RMs that conducted an exchange system overhaul.

Empirical literature on exchange system upgrades and the subsequent firm impact is scarce but still provides valuable insights on the difficulties arising in evaluating exchange system overhauls. Among the first, [2] evaluate the effect of an exchange system upgrade at Deutsche Börse in 2007. However, they rely only on a pre-to-post event comparison of the respective measures. Therefore, observed effects could not entirely be attributed to the update but may instead arise from trends within the time series like monthly growth or changes within the German economy (announcement of employment or trade developments). [14] use multiple pre-event benchmark periods to evaluate the introduction of a new exchange system at the Tokyo stock exchange.

As they use a similar methodology, they do not take into account this possible bias.

Due to our recent sample and the advanced fragmentation of the European order flow, we are able to overcome this drawback by benchmarking exchanges' trading statistics with trading activities at the closest competitor on a day by day basis. In this setup, we benchmark trading volumes of the same shares traded on two trading venues, covering an identical period of time, where one of both RMs introduced an exchange system upgrade. With this methodology we are able to explicitly differentiate between normal time effects within our pre- and post-event window (trend) and the additional abnormal event effects only observable at the exchanges pursuing the exchange system upgrade. Therefore, we are able to evaluate the exchange system upgrade effect more efficiently.

3.2   Dataset

Within our study, we focus on the traded volumes within each exchange's major stock market index (SMI at SIX; OBX at OB). As the biggest European competitors primarily claimed stake in the most liquid stocks, competition is considered most intensive within these indices [18]. We use Thomson Reuters Tick History (TRTH) times and sales data to obtain daily traded volumes for each index constituent at the respective exchange as well as at the most relevant competitor in terms of traded volume: the London-based Bats Chi-X [18].

Relying on traded volumes of the respective exchanges is a key aspect of adequately measuring the direct impact of the IT-investment. In contrast to balance sheet information, traded volumes can be observed in real-time, therefore a potential effect can be analyzed without a time delay between event and day of evaluation which might bias the results due to possible confounding events during this time span. In addition, volume changes at the exchange under consideration are thus directly attributable to the respective exchange system that was overhauled. Nevertheless, within the observation period covering the exchange system upgrade of the SIX, Bats Chi-X finished their infrastructure migration after their merger in late 2011 [21]. However, the major reason for the migration was cost rationalization and the harmonization of the separate infrastructures. Pricing and order routing routines remain unchanged and, most notably, the two order books remained separate. Therefore, we assume that no biases result from this event. To calculate changes in traded volume as well as possible shifts within both market volumes, we rely on the comparison of 50 trading days (holidays are omitted) before and after the upgrade. Table 1 shows the descriptive statistics for our aggregated sample.

Table 1. Descriptive statistics of the datasets

	SMI		OBX	
	SIX	Bats Chi-X	OB	Bats Chi-X
Index constituents	20		25	
Analyzed constituents	19		23	
Observations	1,900		2,300	
Event Date	23.04.2012		12.11.2012	
Pre-Event				
Mean Volume	2,268,137	743,730	3,081,744	484,497
Post-Event				
Mean Volume	2,586,350	777,299	3,456,358	453,253
Pre-Event Volume Correlation	0.9424		0.6371	

Due to the availability of TRTH end-of-day data, we are not able to analyze all index constituents, however, within each index, we account for more than 92 % of the stocks available. Most interestingly, all venues show a rise in the aggregated average trading volume after the exchange system upgrade. However, the same applies for traded volume at Bats Chi-X and seems to be not directly affected by the upgrade. As expected, we observe a high correlation in the daily volume between the respective RM and Bats Chi-X. Trading patterns as well as volume reactions to newly released information are very similar on both venues and therefore trading activity at the competitor will act as a promising benchmark. The resulting market share series are depicted for SIX within Fig. 1 and for the OB in Fig. 2.

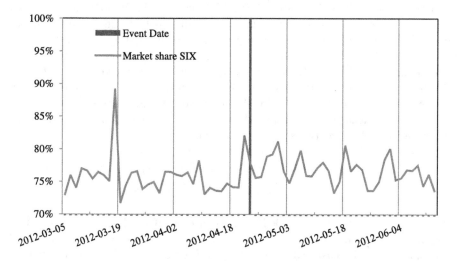

Fig. 1. Market share of the regulated market SIX.

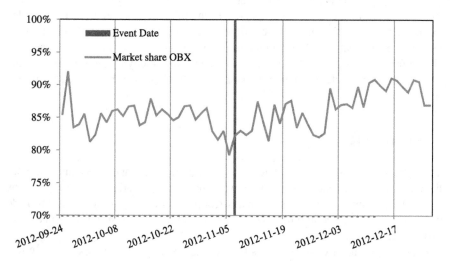

Fig. 2. Market share of the regulated market OB.

3.3 Regression Setup

In order to analyze the effect of the exchange system overhauls on traded volumes, we regress the RM's volume on the respective closest competitor's (Bats Chi-X) volume. Subsequently, the coefficient on Bats Chi-X volume indicates the average aggregated volume distribution between both venues over the observation period. Due to the high pre-event correlation of volumes, we attribute systematical changes in this distribution to the exchange system upgrade by marking the post-event period. Via this stock-specific benchmark, we account for all instrument-specific information and changes in the pre- and post-period, which will be reflected in a high R^2. Fixed-effects transformation is used to eliminate all time-constant heterogeneity between the index constituents and to allow for instrument-specific constants. We further include a full set of time dummies to capture additional time-sensitive but instrument-homogeneous effects. In order to highlight a possible effect caused by the upgrade, we test for a structural break by means of a chow-test [19]. A dummy switching from zero to one after the day of implementation indicates a systematic shift in the volumes at the RM after the event. Likewise, an interaction term between this dummy and the Bats Chi-X volume indicates a possible shift within the volume distribution of both venues, i.e. the sole effect the exchange system upgrade has on the trading volumes. We run this regression for each of the two samples. The regression takes the following form:

$$
\begin{aligned}
Volume_{it} = &\beta' Volume\_BatsChi_{it} + \delta' Indicator_t \\
&+ \gamma' (Indicator_t * Volume\_BatsChi_{it}) + uit
\end{aligned}
\tag{1}
$$

$Volume_{it}$ accounts for the traded volume on each of the RM, respectively $Volume\_BatsChi_{it}$ for the volume on Bats Chi-X. $Indicator$ is the event-dummy and $(Indicator_t * Volume\_BatsChi_{it})$ the interaction. uit aggregates the idiosyncratic, normal error term. Most interesting, the coefficient on $Indicator$ yields a possible positive or negative change in the RM's volume after the event. However, if this change is indeed exclusively attributable to the exchange system upgrade, i.e. solely affects traded volumes at the RM, this will only be indicated by a significant, structural break at the interaction coefficient γ. Time dummies are not indicated in (1) as they are only included for control reasons. The presence of heteroskedasticity requires to additionally apply stock-wise clustered standard errors. The results will be discussed in the following section.

4 Empirical Results

Our key results are shown in Table 2. We compute mean and maximum variance inflation index to evaluate colinearity between independent variables as suggested by [20]. High maximum correlation originates from the similarity of the event-flag *Indicator* and the time series dummies. However, results remain consistent if *Indicator* or dummies are excluded.

As assumed, traded volume at Bats Chi-X is an excellent benchmark for daily RM volume, indicated by the high explanatory power R^2 throughout all estimations as well

Table 2. Regression results

	SMI		OBX	
	Coef.	t-Stat	Coef.	t-Stat
Volume_BatsChi$_{it}$	2.387	8.26***	7.639	4.74***
Indicator	-296,411	-0.84	-1,269,258	-1.12
*(Indicator$_t$ * Volume_BatsChi$_{it}$)*	0.349	2.10**	2.834	5.86***
Time dummies	Included		Included	
Number of observations	1,900		2,300	
Number of groups	19		23	
Overall R^2	0.8844		0.5975	
Max VIF	50.14		50.64	
Mean VIF	2.02		2.41	

as shown by the persistent significance of *Volume_BatsChi$_{it}$* within all models. We therefore subsume that traded volumes at the RM in SMI stocks are on average 2.387 times the volume at Bats Chi-X (subsequently 7.639 at OBX) at the respective observation period. As the coefficient of the Indicator variable is persistently insignificant throughout all two indices, we can conclude that there are no systematic volume differences between pre- and post-event period on the respective RM. That is, we observe no structural shift in the traded volume at the affected market so far.

However, we observe a significant structural break in the volume relationship between the RM and Bats Chi-X. In both cases, and besides from the high pre-event correlation, volumes on the RM develop significantly more positive relative to the volumes at the competitor. Indicated by the positive coefficient of *(Indicator$_t$ * Volume_BatsChi$_{it}$)*, we observe a rise in the volume multiplicator *Volume_BatsChi$_{it}$* after the event date (*Volume_BatsChi$_{it}$ + (Indicator$_t$ * Volume_BatsChi$_{it}$)*). The event effect on market share can be estimated through the coefficients of *Volume_BatsChi$_{it}$* and *(Indicator$_t$ * Volume_BatsChi$_{it}$)*: trading volume in the SMI (OBX) index at Swiss SIX Exchange (Oslo Børs ASA) has increased by on average 14 % (37 %) in comparison to the pre event volume multiplier. These results indicate that although we do not observe a pre- to post-event increase in traded volume at the affected exchange, the exchange experienced a significant more lenient decline compared to the closest competitor in the observed event window. Based on the high pre-event correlation of the respective volumes, we can conclude that this shift is attributable to the infrastructure upgrade on both exchanges.

5   Conclusion

Measuring the value of IT-investments and investigating the strategic advantage caused by enterprise systems has a long tradition in related research. However, since many studies focus on long-term effects of general IT-based resources, attributing a competitive advantage to single information system is hard, especially with respect to comparing the effect on the relative competitive position against other market participants. We overcome this research gap by focusing on the financial sector, i.e. on exchange operators, since this field of competition eases the measurement of the impact of single IT-investments. As competition in this sector is fierce, the services offered are rather substitutive which also eases related analyses. Exchanges depend on successful IT-systems as these ensure the core functionality of exchanges, i.e. bringing together buy and sell orders on an automatic manner. Especially due to the rise of new technologies like High-Frequency-Trading and ongoing fragmentation, exchanges are put more and more under pressure to invest into new systems. Taking into account the tremendous investments which need to be undertaken to overhaul exchange systems, it is still unclear whether these investments translate into strategic advantages by attracting more trading volume and therefore increasing future revenue.

On the basis of two recent system overhauls in 2012, at the Norwegian Oslo Børs and the SIX Swiss Exchange, we analyze if such investments help these firms to gain a strategic advantage in comparison to their closest competitor. In both cases, we identify measureable benefits caused by the introduction of these exchange system investments. We find an increased relative trading volume on both recently introduced exchange systems. Hereby, we contribute to the research stream on exchange system overhauls by adding a new perspective which was left out in previous research: the effect of a new exchange system on the strategic position of the exchange operating firm. We also contribute to the research stream on the strategic usage of enterprise systems in general. Here, we extend previous research that has only taken into account long time periods to measure the general impact of IT-innovations, by instead investigating the timely impact of single IT-investments. We further extend the previous knowledge by the result that the competitive environment of a firm strongly influences the strategic advantages that might arise in this context.

Within further research, we want to extend our study by focusing on an increased amount of exchange system updates in order to be able to draw and verify more general conclusions from the data. Furthermore, we plan to focus on the impact of such system updates on less-liquid stocks. Finally, our current study can also be extended by investigating market quality parameters and their relation to the quality of a competing market. We also plan to address this in future work.

References

1. Davenport, T.: Putting the enterprise into the enterprise system. Harvard Bus. Rev. **76**(4), 121–131 (1998)
2. Riordan, R., Storkenmaier, A.: Latency, liquidity and price discovery. J. Finan. Markets **15**(4), 416–437 (2012)
3. Hendershott, T., Moulton, P.C.: Automation, speed, and stock market quality: the NYSE's hybrid. Working Paper (2011)
4. Bharadwaj, A.: A resource based perspective on information technology and firm performance: an empirical investigation. MIS Q. **24**(1), 169–196 (2000)
5. Mata, F., Fuerst, W., Barney, J.: Information technology and sustainable competitive advantage: a resource-based analysis. MIS Q. **19**(4), 487–505 (1995)

6. Mithas, S., Tafti, A., Bardhan, I., Goh, J.M.: Information technology and firm profitability: mechanisms and empirical evidence. MIS Q. **36**(1), 205–224 (2012)
7. Melville, N., Kraemer, K., Gurbaxani, V.: Information technology and organizational performance: an integrative model of IT. MIS Q. **28**(2), 283–322 (2004)
8. Brynjolfsson, E., Hitt, L.M.: Beyond the Productivity Paradox. Commun. ACM **41**(8), 49–55 (1998)
9. Dewan, S., Kraemer, K.L.: International dimensions of the productivity paradox. Commun. ACM **41**(8), 56–62 (1998)
10. Belleflamme, P.: Oligopolistic competition, IT use for product differentiation and the productivity paradox. Int. J. Ind. Organ. **19**(1–2), 227–248 (2001)
11. Sussman, A., Tabb, L., Ilati, R.: US Equity High Frequency Trading: Strategies, Sizing and Market Structure. Working Paper (2009)
12. Mizen, M., Rhode, W.: Breaking Down the UK Equity Market: Executable Liquidity, Dark Trading, High Frequency and Swaps, Working Paper (2011)
13. Uno, J., Shibata, M.: Speed of Trade and Liquidity. Working Paper (2012)
14. Jain, P., McInish, T.: Reduced Latency and Market Quality on the Tokyo Stock Exchange. Working Paper (2012)
15. SIX: SIX Swiss Exchange schliesst Upgrade ihrer Handelsplattform ab und führt erfolgreich Co- Location Service für ihre Teilnehmer ein. In: Press Release (2012). http://www.six-swiss-exchange.com/media_releases/online/media_release_201204231806_de.pdf
16. OB: Oslo Børs to migrate to the Millennium Exchange trading platform. In: /Press releases/ Press room/About us/Oslo Børs - Oslo Børs, Press Release (2012). http://www.oslobors.no/ob_eng/Oslo-Boers/About-us/Press-room/Press-releases/Oslo-Boers-to-migrate-to-the-Millennium-Exchange-trading-platform
17. European Commission: Directive 2004/39/EC of the European Parliament and of the Council of 21 April 2004 on markets in financial. Official J. Eur. Union (2004)
18. Fidessa: Fidessa Fragmentation Index (2013). http://fragmentation.fidessa.com
19. Chow, G.C.: Tests of equality between sets of coefficients in two linear regressions. Econometrica **28**(3), 591–605 (1960)
20. Wooldridge, J.: Econometric Analysis of Cross Section and Panel Data. The MIT Press Cambridge, London (2002)
21. Wall Street & Technology: BATS Europe Completes Tech Migration of Chi-Ex - Wall Street & Technology (2012). http://www.wallstreetandtech.com/electronic-trading/bats-europe-completes-tech-migration-of/232901228

Conciliating Exploration and Exploitation at Middle-Manager Level: The Case Study of a European Bank Introducing Big Data

Alberto Palazzesi[✉], Chiara Frigerio, and Federico Rajola

Università Cattolica del Sacro Cuore, Milan, Italy
{alberto.palazzesi,chiara.frigerio,
federico.rajola}@unicatt.it

Abstract. This manuscript examines, in a context of radical innovation, the effectiveness of cross functional teams mediating between exploration and exploitation and the knowledge processes that enable organizational ambidexterity. To do so, we conducted a 9 month case study at one of the biggest European banks which is introducing Big Data technologies to support the activity of its corporate relationship managers. The case study focuses on the relationship between the R&D Department and the ICT services provider of the bank and gives evidences that cross-functional teams involving directly these two poles are not, at the first step, the most effective solution at middle-manager level.

Keywords: Ambidexterity · Knowledge management · Case study · Big data · Banks

1 Introduction

Although academy recognizes that ambidexterity, defined as the capability to perform simultaneously explorative and exploitative innovation, is positively associated to organizational performances [1, 2], it is still largely debated how to achieve it.

According to our theoretical commitment, we subscribe to those authors arguing that ambidexterity can be achieved only when exploration and exploitation are spatially separated in different units [3] and subsequently integrated to synchronize, maintain and build portfolios with explorative and exploitative innovations [3].

Given the importance of the integration methods of these two different "poles", the authors reviewed the literature on the integration mechanisms of structural ambidexterity at different hierarchical level and found out that most of the research has focused at top management rather than middle-manager.

Defined as the glue that keeps the organization together [4]. Although literature However, less attention has been posed at middle-manager level where l.

At this lower hierarchical level, the literature recognizes formal integration mechanisms such as cross-teams to be effective [5] because they favorite the combination between exploration and exploitation and a knowledge exchange [6].

© Springer International Publishing Switzerland 2015
A. Lugmayr (Ed.): FinanceCom 2014, LNBIP 217, pp. 90–105, 2015.
DOI: 10.1007/978-3-319-28151-3_7

This paper contributes to this vein of research by investigating, in context of radical innovation, the effectiveness of cross functional teams mediating between exploration and exploitation and the knowledge processes that enable organizational ambidexterity.

To do so, we selected a Banking Group (named Bankia in the rest of the document) from the European financial industry and analyzed, as case study [8], the introduction of a new CRM system based on Big Data technologies.

Beyond the well-known 3v' definition provided by Gartner, we claim that the term "Big Data" does not simply refer to the organization's capacity to collect and store huge amount of data but refers to the possibility to collect and analyse data with an unprecedented breadth, depth and scale [9]. According to this, Big Data represents a cultural and technological phenomenon [10] that is the combination of revolutionary and evolutionary changes and innovations in different fields (both technical and non-technical) [11].

In the case study proposed, we will see how, during the implementation of such a radical innovation, tensions, deriving from different interests and practices between the R&D Department and BankaSolution (the entity within the group providing ICT services, termed as "BS" in the rest of the manuscript) could not be resolved by cross-functional teams involving R&D and BS employees; on the contrary, independent units, mediating between the two, contributed, at the beginning of the project, to the development of common interests and practices which changed the perception of knowledge from "barrier" to "source" of innovation [12].

This manuscript extends extant literature in the following ways: (i) it contributes to the literature on Big Data by means of a qualitative case study showing how introducing these technologies may be challenging in financial institutions; (ii) it analyzes solutions at middle-manager level to conciliate exploration and exploitation contributing to the structural ambidexterity vein of research; (iii) it contributes theoretically to the ambidexterity literature by adopting a framework which integrates ambidexterity and elements of knowledge management at organizational boundaries theory in a unique and powerful way.

The rest of the manuscript develops as follows; Sect. 2 provides the theoretical background of the paper; Sect. 3 is dedicated to the research methodology while Sect. 4 deals with the case study's presentation. Finally, Sect. 5 discusses the main results and concludes the paper.

2 Theoretical Background

2.1 Ambidexterity: An Overview of the Concept

Although the term "ambidexterity" appeared for the first time in [13], the renewed interest in this concept is attributed to [14] that drew a clear distinction between the concepts of exploration and exploitation; according to [14], exploration refers to terms such as "search", "experimentation", "innovation" while exploitation refers to terms such as "refinement" and "efficiency". [14] argues that the two processes are incompatible because they compete for scarce resources and because they require different capabilities. However, the need of equilibrium between the two is recognized as fundamental for superior organizational performances [14].

Most of the literature on ambidexterity has looked at the organizational performances and highlighted a positive relationship between ambidexterity and outcomes [1, 2]; however, this predominant attention over the performances have somehow limited the attention on how ambidexterity is achieved "in practice" and under which circumstances it is fostered [15, 16].

Scholars recognize three different solutions to solve the tensions between exploration and exploitation. The first one, defined as *sequential ambidexterity*, was proposed by [13] that claimed for the necessity of the firms to shift from periods of exploration to periods of exploitation.

The second solution, defined as *structural ambidexterity*, was proposed by [3] arguing that sequential ambidexterity may be ineffective in case of rapid changes and proposed to separate spatially exploration from exploitation and to perform them simultaneously in different autonomous units within the organization.

The third and most recent approach, defined as *contextual ambidexterity*, was proposed by [17] arguing that, within the same unit, ambidexterity could be achieved by designing contexts in which individuals are free to decide how to divide their time between exploration and exploitation.

From a theoretical perspective, while the first two approaches, founded upon the contingency theory [18, 19], claim for the incompatibility of exploration and exploitation and thus separate them temporally (see *temporal ambidexterity*) or structurally (see *structural ambidexterity*), the third approach, based on the paradox theory [20, 21], treats exploration and exploitation as a unique element ontologically indistinct.

By refusing the paradox theory, we conceptualize ambidexterity according to the structural approach and focus, in the rest of the paper, on how ambidexterity can be achieved.

2.2   Achieving Structural Ambidexterity

The mere coexistence of explorative and exploitative activities in different organizational units represents an important yet insufficient condition for organizational ambidexterity [22]; according to [23], in fact, "the crucial task is not the simple organizational structural decision in which the exploratory and exploitative subunits are separated, but the processes by which these units are integrated in a value enhancing way" [23]. This highlights that coordination and integration are necessary steps to be accomplished to achieve organizational ambidexterity [24, 25].

Within the literature on structural ambidexterity, it is widely accepted that top executives have a key role for the integration of the two poles because top managers ensure strategic coherence and balanced resource allocation [26, 27] and because they are the glue that keeps the organization together managing the tensions arising from exploration (where radical innovation takes place) and exploitation (where incremental innovation takes place) [4]. However, this is not the end of the story; [5], in fact, gave to the fore interesting insights on the antecedents both at senior team level and at *middle-manager level* and found out that informal integration mechanisms should be preferred among senior team members while, at lower hierarchical level, formal organizational mechanisms, such as cross functional teams, are positively related to organizational ambidexterity [5].

If on one side senior team integration allows a balanced resource allocation and a coherent strategic path, organizational integration mechanisms at middle-level management favorite the combination between exploration and exploitation units and a knowledge exchange [6] allowing ambidextrous organizations to simultaneously synchronize, maintain and build portfolios with exploitative and explorative innovations [3]. Among the different mechanisms identified in the ambidextrous literature, cross functional interfaces emerged as highly effective to mediate between structural differences and ambidexterity [5]; according to [28], ambidextrous organizations can use cross functional teams to foster knowledge exchange between exploration and exploitation by cutting the organizational boundaries [29] established to separate explorative and exploitative units. Cross functional teams collect employees from different units [5] with distinct skills and expertise and facilitate each employee to reach a common frame and a global understanding [30]. An interesting example in the literature on the role of these teams is provided by [22] that showed how a newspaper organization used cross teams to overcome differences across the traditional newspaper business units (exploitative-oriented) and the internet publishing (explorative oriented). Similarly, [31] argues that both exploration and exploitation can be managed through semi-autonomous subunits with a small fraction of cross-groups links which would allow for the preservation of variety of knowledge within the organization and the identification of valuable synergies.

2.3   Knowledge Management, Exploitation and Exploration

Managing knowledge is difficult but it is strategic for firms [32] because it provides the basis to achieve and sustain competitive advantages [33].

In this paper we conceptualize knowledge with a practice perspective [7] and so we claim that knowledge is constituted by our engagement in a nexus of interconnected practices [34]). Within this stream of research (opposite to the epistemology of possession), the community of practice literature [35, 36] is a clear example; research in this vein shows that individuals, participating in similar activities, develop shared meanings, common norms and ways of doing things [37]. Hence, according to this perspective, knowledge cannot be transferred like an object but can be translated [37, 38] and recreated in different settings; within two communities of practices, in fact, processes and practices of knowledge creation can be shared to support the recreation of knowledge [39].

Given this dutiful premises, it is recognized, also, that knowledge across boundaries leads to innovation performances [40] and that most of the innovation happens directly at the boundaries between disciplines or specializations [41]. According to this, in the last decade, the relationship between boundaries and knowledge has started to be discussed by scholars [12, 29, 35]. [29] reexamined the problem of knowledge and boundaries by analyzing how to manage knowledge across boundaries in settings where innovation was the outcome required; in particular [29] distinguishes three types of boundaries which he defines as "syntactic", "semantic" and "pragmatic" together with the increasing complexity of knowledge defined as "common language", "common meaning" and "common interests". In a syntactic boundary a common language exists and is shared among the different actors involved; this type of knowledge, however, is created overtime and transferred between actors and, when established, it remains robust and solid as long as the boundary conditions remain stable.

Novelty may somehow change this condition of stability since differences and new dependences have to be identified and understood by the different actors. According to the author, in fact, as novelty increases, the amount of effort required to adequately share and assess knowledge also increases; the aim of this boundary is, thus, to develop a common meaning and to learn about and translate other's knowledge.

Sometimes, this novelty may lead to a situation which does not imply differences in meanings but differences in interests [12]; in this context, defined by the author as "pragmatic boundary", common interests have to be developed and different actors need the ability to share, negotiate and transform each other knowledge: to do so, conflicts in the interests must be recognized and trade-off must be examined.

Following [29], in this manuscript we integrate the theory of knowledge management at organizational boundaries within the framework of structural ambidexterity with the aim of evaluating the effectiveness of organizational integration mechanisms in their attempt to conciliate the different practices embedded in the explorative and exploitative units.

By focusing on contexts in which novelties are introduced (such as Big Data), this exploratory qualitative paper extends extant literature on ambidexterity by examining the relationship between organizational integration mechanisms (such as cross functional teams) and knowledge management processes.

3 Methodology

This paper is underpinned by the interpretative paradigm of social sciences and aims at providing deep insights into "the complex world of lived experience from the point of view of those who live it" [42]; since reality is embedded in the social setting, interpretative researchers interpret the reality through a sense making process rather than a hypothesis testing process.

To purse the objective of the research, an interpretative qualitative case study method was chosen [43]; case study is "an empirical inquiry that aims at investigating a particular and contemporary phenomenon within its real-life context when the boundaries between the phenomenon and the context are not evident" [8][1] suitable for explorative researches aimed at investigating the extent of a particular problem and to generate some initial idea on a certain phenomenon.

---

[1] Although this reference follows a positivistic approach to social sciences, this contribution is really valid for a deep understanding on how to design case studies.

According to this, the qualitative case study method was chosen since (i) it enables the description of a certain situation; (ii) the study of a particular context offers depth and richness data by considering the perspective of social actors [44] (Hamel et al., 1993); (iii) it allows theory development.

To purse the research objectives, a European company from the financial services industry (it will be called "Banka" in the rest of this manuscript) was chosen. Banka was selected for two different reasons; firstly, within the European financial industry, few banks have an R&D Department conducing pure explorative activities (moreover, in the country where the research took place, Banka is the unique bank with an R&D unit). Secondly, Banka has recently worked on cutting edge technologies involving Big Data and biometric systems. This public information allowed us to assume that Banka could be a suitable case study where pure explorative (the R&D Department) and pure exploitative (the IT function) activities could be conducted simultaneously.

Data collection took place at the headquarter of the bank from September 2013 to the end of May 2014 and it is characterized by two different phases: from September to December the authors made a couple of high-level explorative interviews to identify (the most innovative projects within the bank, the activities and projects involving both explorative and exploitative units and, finally, possible further interlocutors. From the beginning of December to the end of May, instead, the researchers joined the R&D Department of the bank to participate and to observe their daily activities.

Data were collected from three different sources: (i) interviews; (ii) observations and (iii) documentations.

With respect to the first source, a total of 46 in depth opened interviews were conducted. Interviews were planned with the different interlocutors and were realized in different offices. According to the topic and to the interviewee, questions could be prepared in advance. However, according to the goal and to the paradigm underpinning the research, interviews were semi-structured with open-ending questions allowing the interviewees to expand on the issues they perceived as important relating to the knowledge exchange between different units.

Twenty three different people involved (partially or fully) in the Big Data project were interviewed; among these, the whole R&D unit of the bank (15 people), four people from the Group CIO Department (including the Chief Technology Officer of the bank), two people from the Corporate Marketing Department (including the Head of the Department), one person from the Commercial Investment Banking of "foreign" subsidiaries, one person from BS (the company providing ICT services for Bankia) and, finally, one external lawyer of the bank were interviewed.

A "snowball" technique was followed: interviewee proposed other members within the organizations who could offer additional insights. Some people were interviewed more than once. This was due to the small amount of resources involved in the project who had to face daily changings and tensions which called for a deeper investigation. The range of respondents provided the opportunity to explore tensions arising within the different units and whether there are differences in the actor's interpretation.

Forty interviews were audiotaped, most of which have been transcribed *verbatim*. For those interviews where it was not possible to record the audio, notes were taken during the interview as well as after their completion.

Twenty three different people were involved from five different Departments: R&D, Group CIO, Finance, Corporate Marketing and BS (the entity within the group providing ICT services).

A part from the interviews, the largest source of data collection relies in the researcher' observations; the bank has given us the opportunity to join (from the 1st December 2013 to the 30th May 2014) the R&D Department allowing the researchers to participate at their internal meetings, to work directly on the projects and to observe people's behaviors; hence, by literally living with the participants and sharing their work life over a period of 6 months, the authors were able to capture consistent data on their behavioral patterns and on the subjective experiences of their organizational reality [45] (Smets et al., 2012).

Finally, during the empirical research phase, we have also collected and analyzed both publicly available data, reports and documentation on the Big Data project.

In synthesis, at the end of the field activity we were able to analyze:

- 46 interviews and 1.300 min of data recording;
- notes on 115 days of daily observations;
- 97 pages of slide and documentation.

To strengthen the methodological rigor of the research, a qualitative data analysis tool named NVivo ® was used to capture, code and report the findings of the case study; in particular, this software allowed the authors to collect data into groups of main codes (tree nodes) and sub-nodes which were continuously refined as long as the data collection and the analysis continued to evolve. This technique, named "open coding" [46], was used in the first stage of the data analysis to "open up" the text and find out meanings and ideas.

4 Results

4.1 Case Overview

Banka is one of the biggest European commercial bank groups and serves more than 40 million customers (both retails and businesses) through its 8.000 branches located all over the European countries. Banka employs more than 120.000 people and has an intermediation margin higher than 50 billion euro per year (data at 2013).

Efficiency and innovation are two keywords for Banka's top-management. If, on one side, the recent crisis has pushed the bank to rationalize branches and activities and to increase its operations efficiency (the COO of the bank is trying to maximize the standardization of processes, activities and technologies), on the other side, innovation is getting more and more central for the bank because it represents one of the funda-mental leverages to foster its growth in the countries where it operates.

According to this, the bank is looking to simultaneously balance innovation and efficiency trying to achieve the what so called "ambidextrous behavior". The units dealing with explorative and exploitative activities are briefly introduced in the next two subparagraph.

R&D Department. The R&D Department, in staff to the bank's CEO, is born with the aim of proposing new solutions to the market and to develop innovative ideas using the most cutting edge technologies. Today, it employees 16 individuals with different background ranging from psychology, design, engineering, mathematics and physics.

The way the Department works is particularly innovative within the banking context (traditionally "conservative" and highly formalized); the following quote by the Head of the Department gives a bright picture of their working method: *"Here it is a big mess, we do not have a method of working...(laughing)! No, we do things very horizontally, if I say that there are rules it is just a bit posh. Ideas must come from anybody, anywhere and anyway.. What I am saying now may sound in two different ways: like a thing very free, cool, Silicon Valley or a big mess. We do not want to waste time in doing project management since 50 % of our time would go away on that with no impact on the final result".*

To sum up, the work of this small Department is not particularly structured but the small number of people and the physical closeness among the employees guarantee a discrete level of coordination.

BS. It results from the integration of 13 entities within the Group and it is dedicated mostly to the supply of ICT, Back Office and Middle Office services. The objective of BS is to consolidate and reorganize the operating activities necessary to the business of the group by optimizing operating costs. BS employees today more than 12.000 people in more than 10 countries worldwide and it is highly structured and vertical. Due to its huge size, decisions and activities require long time before getting accepted. BS is defined by the employees of the bank as the "factory" of the Group where all the projects need to converge and be deployed to both the external and internal customers.

4.2 Babel: The New CRM Built upon Big Data Technologies

The financial crisis has definitely contributed to the non-achievement of the business results planned by the bank for the period 2010–2015 but it is not the unique explanation. Bankia's top management has recognized, in fact, that the roots of the negative results derive mainly from the corporate business and, in particular, from the wrong and not effective behaviors of the bank relationship managers that, instead of thinking at a customer in an holistic way, have always worked at *"silos"* and concentrated just on pushing the volumes.

According to this, the management of the bank started to look at solutions which could offer to the corporate relationship managers an holistic view on their customers in terms of client's network, economic conditions of the network and on the overall profitability. Hence, the management of some subsidiaries (where the business's problems were more accentuated) begun to look at external vendors to find a dashboard with the characteristics discussed above. In the meantime these executives, by means of monthly top management meeting, found out that, within the group at holding level, at the R&D's "laboratory", some engineers and mathematician had already started to work on a project, named Babel, to support the corporate relationship managers of the bank.

Babel can be imagined as a dashboard that gives to the user a clear and bright picture of corporate customers. After that the customer relationship manager edits the name of the entity he is interested in, some servers start to examine and process terabytes of data from the datacenter of the bank. A part from the typical financial and economic documents regarding the company, any risk management indicator (PD, LGD, Rating, etc.), the exposition towards the bank according to the type of credit (secured/unsecured loans, advances against discounted invoices, etc.), recent news referred to the company gathered from the web, the most innovative feature of this dashboard revolves around the possibility to see the company within its business network.

Central to the development of this dashboard is, in fact, the concept of the business as a network; according to the Head of R&D: *"It is not important to simply understand whether the financial data of the company are good or not. It is also important to understand what are the overall conditions of the stakeholders of your clients and the financial relationship between your client and its suppliers and customers. This matter because in the other companies there may be some employees with some loans with our bank so, if our client defaults, all the connection may go into default with possible damages for both the supply chains and the employees".*

This dashboard, in fact, allows any relationship manager to see in real time the network of entities of the businesses in its portfolio (raw material's suppliers, customers, etc.). Being drawn as bubbles revolving around the company, the size and the proximity of each bubble indicate how much central is that entity for the Banka's client. Moreover, for those entities which are also clients of Banka, Babel indicates what is their economic and financial conditions by drawing them with different colors ranging from green to red.

This instrument becomes powerful because the customer relationship managers will have a real holistic view of their portfolio and will base their evaluation not only on the economic data of the customer but also on the value of the corporate's network.

When Babel will be "in production", a big amount of data will be continuously downloaded from Banka's Data Warehouses with the aim of giving to the customer relationship-managers the most up-dated picture of their customers. To enable the opportunities described above, Big Data Technologies were adopted. The key differentiating element of these technologies is the use of Open standards built on an open source framework: the 'Hadoop ecosystem'. This ecosystem is composed among others by HDFS (Distributed Filesystem), HBase (no-sql key value store) and Mapreduce (distributed data processing). The use of these new and cutting-edge technologies provides (i) cheap horizontal scalability with increasing of data historical depth and without downgrading performances; (ii) parallel computing and parallel query capability for aggregation and analysis of large amount of data; (iii) response speed, fast loading pages and data access and (iv) resilient distributed architecture.

4.3   The Evolution of Babel from a Knowledge and Organizational Perspective

The Initial (Failing) Phase. Once that the R&D and the business had found a solution to develop Babel in terms of ideas, contents and data, R&D started to work both on the architectural and software side and installed on its servers all those Big Data technologies discussed above with the maximum degree of freedom.

Approximately at the end of 2013, R&D was able to show to the top executives a demo version of the project running in "batch". Banka's top management (CEO and COO) was highly excited to use such technologies because of their low prices, high performances and to the potential effects that it may have at business level. Moreover this project would have been used as the first attempt to introduce Big Data's culture for future projects involving such technologies within the Group.

However, that demo version was miles away from a version which could be run by the systems of the bank with appropriate performances, security levels and stability. To do so, the engagement of BS was necessary because, within the Banking Group, it is the only one entitled to put into production the ideas and the *desiderata* of the business.

Unfortunately, that excitement was not particular accentuate in BS; some managers considered Big Data as a buzzword invented by external vendors to sell something which is useless for the banking context. According to the Head of Global Enterprise Services and Governance of CFO and CRO: *"Big Data is just a trendy name. I am not interested in that. My aim is to give to my CRO and to my CFO consistent data. High quality data is my concern. I am in interested in what the authority and regulators say. I would never start a project on that since banks need something different".*

Vice versa, the Head of Service Line ICT of BS revealed: *"I think that Big Data has to be introduced in bank. We have started to work with Hadoop with the guys of the R&D. But you know what?! Some of my employees face some difficulties. They are used to work in a standardized way since many years and with extant reliable technologies. So I fear we have to overtake a cultural barrier if we want to introduce this highly potential instrument".*

While the R&D was working on its demo version, part of BS's intelligence was moved to the holding and a new unit, named Group CIO (GCIO from now on), was created. Unfortunately, most of the people who moved from BS to GCIO were the ones who, in BS, were favorable to Big Data.

Once that the spin-off BS-Group CIO took place, R&D needed (from January on) to find out potential partners in BS who could be involved in the project. Different meetings took place where the R&D managers tried to explain to BS's managers the features of Babel including: the *desiderata* of the business, the architecture (both physical and logical) and the software application adopted. Babel received few attention since it implied such a different way of working and new competences and knowledge. Discussions took place and BS posed several barriers to this project. According to an employee of the bank previously hired in BS: *"Changes are not easily accepted where there are old-style people. But that place* (talking about BS) *makes you to become like this. Because spending every day in doing maintenance or doing little evolutions doesn't help you to become open-minded. And, another things, there are competence centers that have such things to do...that if you add something then you create frictions. And it is what we found there".*

Hence, initial meetings and formal cross functional teams resulted in a failure. There was no way of working together since distances in terms of competences and interests were too high to be overcome. According to the Head of R&D: *"At the beginning the R&D Department was "risking" to collaborate with such that structure*

(BS) *which was born with the aim of doing the opposite to what we do. So, initially, we were scared to be stopped due and so decided to talk with our top management....".*

Top Management Impulse and New Integrating Mechanisms. At that moment, Babel was stuck since there was no way to find a compromise between R&D and BS. Meeting were useless since the opposite poles were going towards two different strategic directions. Communication was also difficult among the parties since a common dictionary was not possible to be shared.

However, two main impulses emerged. On one side, the business required the immediate development and deployment of the project while, on the other side, the top management decided to promote a new method of working that could enable the collaboration between R&D and BS to allow an ambidextrous behavior during the time; in particular, they decided to install a formal temporary team that could mediate between those two opposite poles. According to this, a group of 5 people from the GCIO where formally appointed as mediating unit. Andrew, from GCIO provided a clear picture of what was happening in that period: *"So there were these 2 worlds which were completely different both in terms of objectives and technologies. R&D works on the most recent technologies, they can't think about" what are the best technology for the day by day maintenance? While BS is the opposite: they don't care about the last functionalities, they care about the running of the applications with the minimum effort...that may be also in terms of maintenance. Whoever arrives, also the external consultants, must be able with a minimum training to make some maintenance on the assets. So two different approaches. Ok, so we arrived at a point in which business said "I want it"! Ok...but who produces it?"*

This situation was resolved by a third external team who mediate between them: *"They came out with this* (referring to the decision of the top management*), so they said "since the gap laboratory-BS is too wide, let's build a middle structure that it is like a bridge". We are this structure. So what is our mission? Our project? On one side we must take all the technical-functional requirements from the R&D and move them to BS...but not tout court. ",* added Paul from Group CIO.

Once that this team from GCIO was officially involved in the project, it started to work hand by hand with R&D team. By physically working 2 days and half per week at the R&D office, they started to learn what the R&D had done, the logics underneath the architectural part of the system and the logic through which algorithms were written. The R&D begun to explain the technologies upon which the whole system was built to this team who had no competence or previous experience in this field. The work of GCIO team was hence to (i) learn these new technologies; (ii) understand (basing on their experiences in BS) which features could be accepted or not; (iii) decide what to propose *tout court* to BS; (iv) translate this knowledge to BS for the industrialization. According to one employee from the Group CIO: *"One thing that we must do is trying to reduce the criticalities because of the last technologies. So what is possible to do? What has to be cut? It was done to reduce the impact on the factory....because BS thinks with technologies which are 12 years old".*

According to this, Group CIO started twice a week to work also with a team from BS. Observing directly this working groups, it clearly emerged the attitude of the BS to complain when an higher degree of innovation was required. However, it was interesting to notice how Group CIO employees were better at interacting with their ex-colleagues due to their past experience and to their perception of what was feasible or not.

Hence, knowledge started to flow from the R&D to GCIO and from GCIO to BS where no prior knowledge on Big Data was present.

Meetings between Group CIO and BS lasted for a couple of months. Some decisions were taken about the elements to use and abolish with respect to the first demo done by the R&D. Decisions were then exported to the R&D team that started to work at a new functioning prototype of Babel used (July, 2014) by a sample of 400 customer relationship managers.

Today the project has not been industrialized yet, but the logics and an overall knowledge on Big Data is perfectly shared across the R&D, the Group CIO and BS who is beginning its industrialization phase. With respect to the first initial idea, many changes have been done. This is not due simply to the resistance of the "factory" but has its roots also in the way Babel was initially realized. Within the period spent with these working groups, a metaphor from the automotive car was often used; R&D has built a beautiful, fast and revolutionary car which can be shown at the Geneva's exposition and used in a racetrack for a couple of laps; however, this car can't be produced in big volumes for two main reasons: (i) it would be highly inefficient since it is difficult to standardize within a factory line; (ii) there is the risk that after 10 km the engine breaks or that the clutch may have some problems.

The mediation of the Group CIO unit resulted in a success. Firstly, it enabled the industrialization of Babel. Secondly, it has contributed to create a global know-how about Big Data also in BS. Thirdly, this intermediation allowed R&D and BS to find a way of interacting with each other. In the last period, in fact, the BS's team following Babel went to work directly at the R&D laboratory to share ideas, comments and opinions to improve the overall performances of the final product.

5   Discussion and Conclusions

The aim of this study is twofold; on one side, authors wants to examine, in a context of radical innovation, the effectiveness of cross functional teams mediating between exploration and exploitation and, on the other side, the knowledge processes that enable organizational ambidexterity [6]. In order to accomplish this goal, a 9 months study was conducted at a European commercial bank which is trying to introduce Big Data technologies within its existing information systems.

According to the outcomes presented in the previous paragraph, the project could be split into three different phases. In the initial phase, two main actors were involved: (i) the R&D, a small and "organic" unit dealing with "experimentation", "innovation" [14] and knowledge creation; (ii) BS which is a big, "mechanic" entity dealing with "efficiency", "production" [14] and knowledge refinement. Using the words suggested by the ambidextrous framework, the first phase was characterized by one explorative unit and by one exploitative unit [3, 47].

Although these two units are separated in the space and highly differentiated [19], at a certain point, integration was required since the product (the CRM interface based on Big Data technologies) could not been put into production (by BS) unless knowledge would have been exchanged across the different units. Knowledge exchange was also promoted by the management of Banka since the aim of this first project on Big Data was also to create an initial culture on these technologies and to create synergies between who is entitled for the innovation and who is entitled for its deployment and "production" [4].

Cross functional teams including employees from both the poles were thus formally appointed to reach a common understanding and to align the interests of both [30, 37].

However, this initial phase resulted in a complete failure since cross-functional teams were not able to mediate between exploration and exploitation due to (i) a conflict of interests between the R&D the BS managers, (ii) high degree of novelty embedded in Big Data which required a common lexicon to be identified [29]. This indicates us that, this integrating mechanism can be weak because of the different practices, activities and norms embedded in exploitative and explorative units and because of their divergent interests [29].

However, this initial difficulty was subsequently solved by the top management that, with the aim of conciliating exploration and exploitation between the different organizational boundaries, formally appointed a third organizational unit to mediate between R&D Department and BS: GCIO.

The success of this mediation relies in the physical proximity of some of its employees both to R&D and to BS. Two parallel cross functional teams were, in fact, instituted and involved, on one side, R&D-GCIO and on the other side, GCIO-BS with the objective to find a global and common frame of interests (define by [29] as "pragmatic boundary"). Once that a common frame was individuated and knowledge got transformed, GCIO begun the following knowledge management process: it started to translate knowledge from R&D to Group CIO with the aim of defining a common language and identifying common norms (this is what [29] would call "semantic boundary") [12, 29]. The success of this mediating unit relies in the fact that all the employees came from BS which allowed this group to make knowledge flowing in a most powerful way.

Once that common lexicon, norms and practices [29] were established, R&D and BS managed to directly institute cross-functional teams to begin the industrialization of the project (in this case we deal with the syntactic boundary [29]).

According to this, a second insight emerges from the research; cross functional teams involving independent organizational units may favor the work of future cross-functional teams involving people from the explorative and the exploitative pole.

In conclusion, from the evidences of the case study we argue that embedded practices and divergent interests may have a negative impact on the effectiveness of cross functional teams involving directly employees from the explorative and the exploitative poles. However, this mechanism becomes powerful (in line with [9, 22, 31]) after that common interests and meanings are recreated by independent units that keep, at the beginning, the two poles separated.

This study is prone to some limitations which could be tackled in future investigations. Firstly, the single case study methodology may be objectionable because it allows no generalization unless it represents a unique and specific situation [8]. However, this is somehow defensible since few studies on structural ambidexterity were based on financial institutions with R&D Departments. According to this, it would be interesting to present to the fore multiple case studies to evidence differences and similarities. In particular, within the financial industry it may be interesting to compare cases from different countries or institutions with different sizes; in this paper we analyzed a big, highly structured and bureaucratic bank and we think that different evidences may emerge from smaller and agiler institutions. Secondly, this study can be considered somehow as incomplete since the project has not been industrialized yet. However 9 months of data collecting and 6 months of daily observations gave us a sufficient (but not exhaustive) dataset to describe how challenging is to implement such technologies within big-size financial institutions.

References

1. He, Z.L., Wong, P.K.: Exploration vs. exploitation: an empirical test of the ambidexterity hypothesis. Organ. Sci. **15**(4), 481–494 (2004)
2. Hill, S.A., Birkinshaw, J.: Ambidexterity and survival in corporate venture units. J. Manage. 10.1177/0149206312445925 (2012)
3. Tushman, M.L., O'Reilly III, C.A.: Ambidextrous organizations: managing evolutionary and revolutionary change. Calif. Manage. Rev. **38**(4), 8–30 (1996)
4. O'Reilly, C.A., Tushman, M.L.: The ambidextrous organization. Harvard Bus. Rev. **82**(4), 74–83 (2004)
5. Jansen, J.J., Tempelaar, M.P., Van den Bosch, F.A., Volberda, H.W.: Structural differentiation and ambidexterity: the mediating role of integration mechanisms. Org. Sci. **20**(4), 797–811 (2009)
6. Tsai, W., Ghoshal, S.: Social capital and value creation: the role of intrafirm networks. Acad. Manage. J. **41**(4), 464–476 (1998)
7. Cook, S.D., Brown, J.S.: Bridging epistemologies: the generative dance between organizational knowledge and organizational knowing. Org. Sci. **10**(4), 381–400 (1999)
8. Yin, R.K.: Case Study Research: Design And Methods (Applied Social Research Methods). Sage Publications, Thousand Oaks (1989)
9. Lazer, D., Pentland, A.S., Adamic, L., Aral, S., Barabasi, A.L., Brewer, D., Van Alstyne, M.: Life in the network: the coming age of computational social science. Science **323**(5915), 721 (2009)
10. Boyd, D., Crawford, K.: Critical questions for big data: provocations for a cultural, technological, and scholarly phenomenon. Inform. Comm. Soc. **15**(5), 662–679 (2012)
11. Gantz, J., Reinsel, D.: Extracting Value from Chaos. IDC iView, pp. 1–12 (2011)
12. Carlile, P.R.: A pragmatic view of knowledge and boundaries: boundary objects in new product development. Org. Sci. **13**(4), 442–455 (2002)
13. Duncan, R.B.: The ambidextrous organization: designing dual structures for innovation. Manage. Org. **1**, 167–188 (1976)
14. March, J.G.: Exploration and exploitation in organizational learning. Org. Sci. **2**(1), 71–87 (1991)
15. Kauppila, O.P.: Creating ambidexterity by integrating and balancing structurally separate interorganizational partnerships. Strat. Org. **8**(4), 283–312 (2010)
16. Durisin, B., Todorova, G.: A study of the performativity of the "Ambidextrous Organizations" theory: neither lost in nor lost before translation. J. Prod. Innovat. Manag. **29**(S1), 53–75 (2012)

17. Gibson, C.B., Birkinshaw, J.: The antecedents, consequences and mediating role of organizational ambidexterity. Acad. Manag. J. **47**(2), 209–226 (2004)
18. Woodward, J., Dawson, S., Wedderburn, D.: Industrial Organization: Theory and Practice, vol. 3. Oxford University Press, London (1965)
19. Lawrence, P.R., Lorsch, J.W., Garrison, J.S.: Organization and Environment: Managing Differentiation and Integration. Division of Research, Graduate School of Business Administration, Harvard University, Boston (1967)
20. Smith, K.K., Berg, D.N.: Paradoxes of Group Life: Understanding Conflict, Paralysis and Movement in Group Dynamics. Jossey-Bass, San Francisco (1987)
21. Cameron, K.S., Quinn, R.E.: Organizational paradox and transformation. Ballinger Publishing Co/Harper & Row Publishers (1988)
22. Gilbert, C.G.: Change in the presence of residual fit: can competing frames coexist? Org. Sci. **17**(1), 150–167 (2006)
23. O'Reilly III, C.A., Tushman, M.L.: Ambidexterity as a dynamic capability: resolving the innovator's dilemma. Res. Org. Behav. **28**, 185–206 (2008)
24. Smith, W.K., Tushman, M.L.: Managing strategic contradictions: a top management model for managing innovation streams. Org. Sci. **16**(5), 522–536 (2005)
25. Gupta, A.K., Smith, K.G., Shalley, C.E.: The interplay between exploration and exploitation. Acad. Manage. J. **49**(4), 693–706 (2006)
26. Lubatkin, M.H., Simsek, Z., Ling, Y., Veiga, J.F.: Ambidexterity and performance in small-to medium-sized firms: the pivotal role of top management team behavioral integration. J. Manage. **32**(5), 646–672 (2006)
27. Jansen, J.J., George, G., Van den Bosch, F.A., Volberda, H.W.: Senior team attributes and organizational ambidexterity: the moderating role of transformational leadership. J. Manage. Stud. **45**(5), 982–1007 (2008)
28. Gupta, R., Govindarajan, V.: Knowledge flows within multinational corporations. Strat. Manage. J. **21**, 473–495 (2000)
29. Carlile, P.R.: Transferring, translating, and transforming: an integrative framework for managing knowledge across boundaries. Org. Sci. **15**(5), 555–568 (2004)
30. Daft, R.L., Lengel, R.H.: Organizational information requirements, media richness and structural design. Manage. Sci. **32**(5), 554–571 (1986)
31. Fang, C., Lee, J., Schilling, M.A.: Balancing exploration and exploitation through structural design: the isolation of subgroups and organizational learning. Org. Sci. **21**(3), 625–642 (2010)
32. Easterby, S.M., Prieto, I.M.: Dynamic capabilities and knowledge management: an integrative role for learning?*. Brit. J. Manage. **19**(3), 235–249 (2008)
33. Grant, R.M.: Toward a knowledge based theory of the firm. Strat. Manage. J. **17**(S2), 109–122 (1996)
34. Nicolini, D.: Practice as the site of knowing: insights from the field of telemedicine. Org. Sci. **22**(3), 602–620 (2011)
35. Brown, J.S., Duguid, P.: Organizational learning and communities-of-practice: toward a unified view of working, learning, and innovation. Org. Sci. **2**(1), 40–57 (1991)
36. Lave, J., Wenger, E.: Situated Learning: Legitimate Peripheral Participation. Cambridge University Press, Cambridge (1991)
37. Orr, J.E.: Talking about Machines: An Ethnography of a Modern Job. Cornell University Press, London (1996)
38. Gherardi, S.: Organizational Knowledge: The Texture of Workplace Learning. Wiley, New York (2009)
39. Bresnen, M., Goussevskaia, A., Swan, J.: Organizational routines, situated learning and processes of change in project-based organizations. Proj. Manage. J. **36**(3), 27–42 (2005)

40. Cohen, W.M., Levinthal, D.A.: Absorptive capacity: a new perspective on learning and innovation. Admin. Sci. Quart. **35**(1), 128–152 (1990)
41. Leonard, D.: Wellspring of Knowledge. Harvard Business School Press, Boston (1995)
42. Schwandt, T. A.: Constructivist, interpretivist approaches to human inquiry (1994)
43. Walsham, G.: Interpretive case studies in IS research: nature and method. Eur. J. Inform Syst. **4**(2), 74–81 (1995)
44. Hamel, J., Dufour, S., Fortin, D.: Case study methods, vol. 32. Sage, Thousand Oaks (1993)
45. Smets, M., Morris, T.I.M., Greenwood, R.: From practice to field: a multilevel model of practice-driven institutional change. Acad. Manage. J. **55**(4), 877–904 (2012)
46. Strauss, A., Corbin, J: Open coding. In: Basics of Qualitative Research: Grounded Theory Procedures and Techniques, vol. 2, pp. 101–121 (1990)
47. Benner, M.J., Tushman, M.L.: Exploitation, exploration and process management: the productivity dilemma revisited. Acad. Manage. Rev. **28**(2), 238–256 (2003)

Seasonality and Interconnectivity Within Cryptocurrencies - An Analysis on the Basis of Bitcoin, Litecoin and Namecoin

Martin Haferkorn[✉] and Josué Manuel Quintana Diaz

Goethe University Frankfurt, Theodor-W.-Adorno-Platz 4, Frankfurt/Main, Germany
haferkorn@wiwi.uni-frankfurt.de, jq.diaz@icloud.com

Abstract. The market development of cryptocurrencies illustrates an institutional change how payments can be released and received without the need of any intermediary or trusted central party to clear virtual transactions. As academia focuses mostly on Bitcoin, the increased money demand within cryptocurrencies, its linkages, the wide range of possible channels to release and receive executed payments (payment patterns) and the wide range of different underlying motivations why cryptocurrencies are demanded to release payments (payment behavior) is still uncovered. One might assume that payment patterns and payment behavior converges in the future as soon as the experimenting phase would have cooled down. However we observe that Bitcoin shows a strong, Litecoin a weak and Namecoin no weekday seasonality. By analyzing observed number of payments directly (between these cryptocurrencies) and indirectly (via the Bitcoin exchange-rate) we find no relationship. We conclude on these findings that payment patterns and payment behaviors on the basis of cryptocurrencies Bitcoin, Litecoin and Namecoin continue to diverge.

Keywords: Bitcoin · Cryptocurrencies · Decentralized Transactions · Digital Currency · Litecoin · Namecoin · Payment Behavior · Virtual Money

1 Introduction

Since the introduction of Bitcoin in 2009 by [1] the concept of a decentralized trusted digital currency became quite prominent due to rising media attention on Bitcoin. Caused by the open-source nature of Bitcoin an increasing amount of several descendants could unfold and be experimented within the last years. As of 2014, over 275 of these cryptocurrencies have been developed [2] differing between each other in terms of implementation and design. However they share the same technical design principle based on cryptography to secure trust in decentralized transactions (i.e. cryptocurrency) as proposed in Bitcoin by [1]. Within the uplifting media attention on Bitcoin the advantages of cryptocurrencies are becoming more and

© Springer International Publishing Switzerland 2015
A. Lugmayr (Ed.): FinanceCom 2014, LNBIP 217, pp. 106–120, 2015.
DOI: 10.1007/978-3-319-28151-3_8

more acknowledged, thus gaining more traction in terms of usage and eventually market capitalization [3,4]. While academia has focused mostly on Bitcoin so far little attention has been put towards emerging Bitcoin alternatives, so called alternative or alternate cryptocurrencies (i.e. Altcoins) [5]. With this paper we are among the first in shedding light into the still barely analyzed emerging landscape of Altcoins and virtual transactions, which are decentrally and autonomously organized, as they might become a substantial driver to curb transaction cost of an increasingly computerized market economy. At first we address the basic question how to categorize money demand to differentiate between cryptocurrencies in contrast to established fiat money. We introduce a categorization model to illustrate not only the range of possible channels to execute payments (payment patterns) but also the wide range of different underlying motivations why cryptocurrencies might get demanded to release payments (payment behavior). By analyzing data of the two earliest Bitcoin descendants, Litecoin and Namecoin, which share a very similar technical design, we exploit the unique property of 100 % transparent payments (in terms of quantity and price) to analyze usage patterns. In particular in this paper, we strive to observe if seasonalities of money demand within these currencies to release payments are existent and if payments are interconnected to each other. As these cryptocurrencies share are similar protocol, one might think whether the quantity of payments of these three cryptocurrencies influences each other. Litecoins and Bitcoins might in fact underlie a same trend and correlate with regard to a similar seasonal effects. If so, we argue Litecoins or any similar Altcoin might represents just a replicate, substitutable over time and payment patterns and payment behavior might converge in the future as soon as the experimenting phase would have cooled down. This hypothesis of converging payment patterns and payment behavior within a wide range of cryptocurrencies' might direct towards a cryptocurrency, which might be of most utility for money demand to release payments. This hypothesis will be discussed in this work more thoroughly. Our work is structured as follow: at first we give an overview of the discussion of cryptocurrencies by categorizing money demand, how cryptocurrencies fit into this categories, and how future money demand and payments might get changed due to the increased usage of Peer-to-Peer Computer Networks virtual transaction, which overcome centrally trusted third parties like a bank or a stock exchange to clear transactions between entities. The next section gives an overview about relevant literature in this area followed by a section where our analysis is presented. Our results, concluding remarks along with the limitations are given in the last two sections.

2   Categorization of Money and the Motivation to Demand Bitcoins, Litecoins and Namecoins

Max Weber underlined money as the essential instrument to make the risky adventure of modern capitalism work [6]. Niklas Luhmann described money as constructed medium to communicate, a social glue, which enables economic interactions based on payments in the modern society. Putting this in context: if no payments would be made, the modern economic system as we know would stop to exist [7]. In the dawn of computerization there is an increasingly notably shift of money demanded, from conventional fiat money as for example Euros or USD, towards new forms of money to release payments, like Bitcoins, Litecoins and Namecoins to name only a few.

2.1 "Money is What Money Does" - Categorization of Money

Money can be defined as a symbolic value equivalent. Symbolic because what ever form is used for money it symbolizes something of equivalent value and in doing so entitles someone to claim on scarce resources. Symbolic value equivalents can be an object of economic transactions but are not necessary to execute transactions. Economic transactions are based on economic interactions in terms of "giving and taking resources" from each other. How this giving and taking evolves between persons determines the sort and course of how persons expect to relate to each other. Symbolic value equivalents can either be demanded to serve this established relation and be used as object of economic transactions to release payments, or not.

Following the here outlined categorization model of [8] money, the functionality of money, facilitating economic interactions, can be categorized in terms of the underlying form of economic relation among payee and payer: i.e. (1) relations based on debt (exchanging resources), (2) relations based on unilateral gifts (endowing resources) or (3) relations based on common pooled resources (sharing resources). Thus, "money is what money does" serving either relations based on debt, unilateral gifts or common pool resources. In the following the notion of currency is defined not in the narrow sense, money as recognized legal tender, but as more commonly defined as exchangeable money, exchangeable for example into other currencies of respective equivalent value [10,11]. Likewise, Bitcoin, Litecoin and Namecoin can be categorized as symbolic value equivalents, which serve exchange based relations, which are cleared Person-to-Person, or rather Peer-to-Peer (P2P), are non-physical and thus purely virtual in nature. All three virtual coins are based on a cryptographic protocol (i.e. cryptocurrency). There is no private or public money issuer involved. All money issuance, its distribution and circulation is decentralized within a common P2P-network operating autonomously without any central point of control and single point of failure. This allows trust-free transactions, storage and control of newly created coins. In other words each cryptographic protocol represents a virtual, fully autonomously operating Central Bank, which adheres to the intractable rules set in the protocol.

2.2 What do Cryptocurrencies Have in Common

There are four particularities, which all cryptocurrencies share in common [9]: (i) first, they all are virtual in nature. (ii) Second, the quantity is fixed not the price. (iii) Third, they rely on a self-organized computer network (P2P), which self-enforces transactions of any kind. Thus, cryptocurrencies share features of a global currency area based on its own terms and conditions to execute transactions. (iv) Fourth, they represent all in fact an equity share of a virtual organization, which operates decentralized and autonomously - changing the nature how firms might operate in the future to economize on transaction costs. (i) Cryptocurrencies share features of a digitalized symbolic value equivalent. Whether a cryptocurrency - which acts as virtual value equivalent and abstractions of value - is valuable or not, lays, like in the case of any symbolic value equivalents, in the eye of the demander of money. Or more technically precise in the case of cryptocurrency lays in the eyes of the keyholder. In other words cryptocurrency, as all other virtual value equivalents, do not physically exist, there are only records of transactions on a decentralized and autonomously organized ledger [12]. In the case of Bitcoins the ledger is represented by a chain of blocks, called blockchain. (ii) Cryptocurrencies share features of a commodity: i.e. the quantity and not the price (face value) is fixed at issuance. Thus, in the case of a commodity, supply is bounded and cryptocurrency and its underlying coins can be considered as digital commodity money. The cryptocurrency is valuable not only due to its scarcity but also due to the increasing demand fostered by the network effect. (iii) Cryptocurrencies share features of a new way to ensure the organizations of transactions based on a computer protocol (i.e. algorithm), which enables decentralized transactions without the need to trust any counterparty or any entrusted third party. In other words a cryptographic computer protocol on which cryptocurrencies are based share features of a Decentralized Autonomous Organisations (DAOs), which offer services on basis of self-enforcing transactions allowing to complete transactioncs trust free and programmable. (iv) Cryptocurrencies share features of equity, where a cryptocurrency holder becomes in fact a stockholder of the DAO and can use their equity stocks as value equivalent to buy services offered by the computer controlled organization. The outside view of a DAO is a cryptocurrency, backed by the value of the services, which a particular DAO provides. In the case of Namecoin it is for example it is to register an own domain based on the Top-Level Domain "bit". In addition to this the cryptocurrency holder, is entitled as co-owner of the DAO to the profits, due to price increases, that the DAO receives from providing services, which are increasingly demanded. Same is true for losses. In other words Namecoins either appreciate or depreciate relatively in value.

In a nutshell, cryptocurrency can be seen as digital commodity money, which is monetized and managed by a common P2P network, without any prior relationship or trust between persons, and without the need to trust the direct counterparty or a centralized trusted authority as counterpart. A common pool resource, which is organized by a purely distributed trust-free network to release and receive payments. The only trust, which remains to release and receive payments, is trust in the integrity of the algorithm and the incorruptness of the cryptographic secured ledger.

2.3   What is Differences Between Bitcoin, Litecoin and Namecoin

The counterparty risk of a centralized third party can be overcome by a decentralized electronic ledger. In theory any thinkable virtual transaction can be decentralized on-blockchain and by this avoid transaction costs and risks of any controlling authority. The central question is to build either (i) an independent network based on an own consensus protocol or to build (ii) a protocol on top of Bitcoin's protocol. In the following the platform Namecoin and Litecoin serve as an example of either of the two possibilities: Namecoin represents like Litecoin an alternate cryptocurrency (i.e. Altcoin). The difference between Namecoin and Litecoin however is that the Namecoin blockchain builds on the same algorithm like Bitcoin does, however not based directly on the Bitcoin protocol but on an own protocol. In contrast the Litecoin blockchain represents an independent common network, which is based on an own protocol with the goal to make transactions significantly faster and mining more cost-effective and resource-efficient. Litecoin provides a transaction confirmation duration of 2,5 min on average. In Bitcoin it takes 10 min on average. Another difference represents the scheduled cap of supplied coins. Litecoin schedules 84 million coins, whereas Bitcoin caps supply at 21 million coins.

2.4   Namecoin as First Backed Cryptocurrency

Namecoin can be considered as first big strand of Altcoins, which became created in 2010 and can be described as decentralized name registration database on-blockchain. In other words namecoin represents a top level domain (TLD) address ending with ".bit", which can be bought and sold, and thus can be considered both as sort of backed cryptocurrency and a non-fungible but tradable asset. Not the Internet Corporation for Assigned Names and Numbers (ICANN) takes control and monetizes the Domain Name System (DNS) but users within the bitcoin network control and monetize person-to-person domain names. Like in the case of the Bitcoin network the confirmation time averages 10 min and the supply of coins is capped at 21 millions coins. In other words a limited number of ".bit" TLD addresses can be distributed. In contrast to Bitcoin and many other Altcoins Namecoin represents a backed virtual currency, backed by a scarce resource in terms of an unique ".bit" TLD address.

2.5   Decentralized Organizations of Virtual Transactions
        and Payments

The current market developments in decentralizing the organizations of transactions and payments remains disruptive and likely to take-off and accelerate further as network externalities become stronger. The characteristic of Namecoin or other Altcoins in general illustrate the wide range of other forms of transactions which can be build on-blockchain [12]. For example, to mark cryptocurrencies, which separate them from the rest of the coins ("colored coins"). "Colored coins" are trackable and can be used as special purpose currency for certain transactions only with own value, or even as special purpose vehicle to refer to single assets or a portfolio of assets of any kind. "Colored coins" could be used as well to refer to property entitlements of any kind ("smart property") ready to use for all sort of virtual transactions and economic interactions (e.g. decentralized exchanges, gifts or commonly pooled resources). This works respectively in the case to constrain choice by commonly agreed rules based on a contract without the need of a trusted third party, e.g. to cash out money if parties adhered successfully to the agreed rules ("smart contracts"), or even follow a commonly agreed set of rules to organize, i.e. so called Decentralized Anonymous Organizations (DAO). The wide range of possible virtual transactions and payments, which can be organized by a decentralized-trusted ledger, illustrates two features, which will be analyzed in the following sections more thoroughly. (i) First, the wide range of possible channels to execute payments in the future. And (ii) second the wide range of different motivations why symbolic value equivalents in form of decentralized digital commodity money (cryptocurrencies) might be demanded to release payments, or not. It is reasonable to assume that due to the similarity of the implementation and technical design of Litecoins and Bitcoins that they might underlie a same trend and correlate with regard to a similar seasonal effects. Namecoins are as well derived in the exact way as Bitcoins, even the same hardware to mine coins can be used for both, however differ in terms of the functionality by offering a service of a top level domain address. Thus Litecoins and Bitcoins might not be interconnected as much to Namecoin as among themselves and thus might be significantly uncorrelated in terms of price and quantity movements (i.e. payments).

3   Literature Review

As stated within our introduction most of the academic work is as of 2014 based on the (by market capitialization) largest and oldest cryptocurrency Bitcoin. In this regard we devote our research here on Altcoins as well. As we analyze the factors which drive the quantity of payments within these cryptocurrency we present literature which relates towards explaining these factors, i.e. behavioral and technological research in this field. Beforehand we also give a short summary on the small literature on cryptocurrencies.

3.1   Cryptocurrencies

Research on cryptocurrencies in general and the connection between the currencies is as of 2014 quite uncovered as academia focuses mostly on Bitcoin. [13] tries to explain while cryptocurrencies are yet not widespread adapted. He concludes on the basis of economic model by [14] that network effects and switching costs for the majority of the population is to high. [15] analyze the market capitalization between different cryptocurrencies. In their study they focus on six cryptocurrencies (including Litecoin and Namecoin). They find that the exchange-rate of other cryptocurrencies do not profit within the first period of their dataset (May-September 2013) as the Bitcoin exchange-rate outperforms these other cryptocurrencies. In contrast the following four month the effect reverses the as the exchange-rate of the other cryptocurrencies compared to USD increased. Additionally they find that triangluar cryptocurrency arbitrage is hardly possible within most exchanges thus the exchange-rates are efficient.

3.2   Bitcoin

Behavioral Research Stream. Research on the behavior aspects of Bitcoin can be divided into following areas: (i) the usage of Bitcoin (ii) analyzing the factors which influence the exchange-rate between Bitcoin and fiat money.

(i) [26] are among the first who provide an insight into transactions between the introduction of Bitcoin 2009 and 2012. They find that the most new generated Bitcoins are left within the account, contrary to this they also observe many small transactions. [17] argues that Bitcoin only can be used as currency within communities. Therefore he dismisses that Bitcoin can be seen as a realistic alternative to classic currencies. [18] concludes on the Basis of a correlation analysis that Bitcoin can not be merely defined as currency but more as a speculative asset. Evidence on the basis of a behavioral analysis backing this argument is provided by [19]. They showed that the exchange volume between USD and Bitcoin does not translate into an increase in the quantity of payments within the Bitcoin network, an indication that Bitcoin is used as speculative asset.

(ii) As shown in the previous section the usage of Bitcoin as an actual currency was dismissed, further due to the fact the Bitcoin itself does not inherit an interest rate mechanism it is of highly interest for academia and investors which factors drive the exchange-rate. One factor which could be identified by several studies is the number of search queries on Google and article views in Wikipedia on the term Bitcoin which increases the exchange-rate [20,21]. [21] further finds that a decrease in the amount of hits in Wikipedia and Google search queries does not translate into a decrease of the exchange-rate. [22] show that the exchange-rate volatility increase along with the exchange-rate.

Technical Aspects. Papers on technical aspects can be divided into papers regarding (1) anonymity within Bitcoin and (2) protocol related research.

(1) Anonymity is a very important motivation to use Bitcoin, thus [23] show in a simulation that users can be mapped passively if they use the same address for their daily transactions. This leads them to the conclusion that using Bitcoin provides only a small level of anonymity. To the same conclusion comes [24] by outlining that users can be mapped passively as they have to interact with centralized service such as currency exchanges and online wallets. [27] note that merging of several Bitcoin input addresses, a common functionality used within Bitcoin, to one output address also decreases anonymity. It can be stated that Bitcoin does not provide a secure level of anonymity, further it should be noted that usage of passive techniques leaves the user clueless if he is probed which makes the situation even worse.

(2) As Bitcoin heavily relates on the information technology it success depends highly on the protocol and the underlying implementation. Especially

double-spending must be prevented. [25] present a scenario where they show that double spending possible, however they refer to the fast payment mode, where payments and not checked against the blockchain. [16] outlines the possibility of a double spending attack if more than 50 % of the network is controlled by an attacker. Due to the fact of the required computer capacity and expected payoff this seems be as of 2014 an unlikely scenario.

4   Research Design

4.1   Research Questions

The question we aim at with our work is whether the payments within the three cypto-currencies Bitcoin, Litecoin and Namecoin follow distinct properties. A research gap which no been addressed within Bitcoin and merely other cryptocurrencies. As current national payment systems do not give academia an insight on these seasonal and inter-usage patters we are among the first to dissect the distinct effects within a real-world payment system. Against this background, our results give an indication when people act between each other trough cryptocurrencies. We also focus on seasonalities which can be observed within many financial systems for example in trading volumes in securities trading [28, 29, 32] and foreign exchange trading [31]. Especially, as humans influence these processes seasonalities can occur within these volumes. However it is still unclear whether these processes also apply to cryptocurrencies as they are artificial and mostly driven by algorithms (e.g. due to money creation). Another factor is that and many different nations (timezones) and cultures (behavior) take part. We strive to gain a first indication if the quantity of payments follow seasonalities like weekdays, month and years. Thus, we ask at first following research question:

RQ1: Seasonality - how do seasonalities influence the quantity of payments within cryptocurrencies?

As outlined in the previous section most cryptocurrencies share the same underlying technology. Therefore one could assume that the behavior exhibited within this network is driven by similar people who are using the cryptocurrency in a same manner. It is obvious that this behavior is reflected within the payment behavior in these cryptocurrencies. Referring again to the financial markets it has been observed that volumes correlate [30]. Consequently one might expect that applies also to cryptocurrencies. An argument against this assumption is the fact that cryptocurrencies have different intended use cases. For example Namecoin has a different intended usage compared to Bitcoin and Litecoin, one might expect that it stands apart from the other cryptocurrencies. In order to resolve this conflicting assumptions we address following second research question:

RQ2: Interconnectivity - does the quantity of payments within a cryptocurrencies influences the quantity of payments within another cryptocurrencies?

4.2 Regression Setup

As shown in Fig. 1 (Sect. 5.1) the quantity of payments of each cryptocurrency has an underlying trend. This property is not unusual and can be observed in many timeseries. Trends can affect both dependent and independent variables which could bias the results if not taken appropriately into account within OLS regressions. One solution to overcome this problem is to compute the difference between two consecutive observations (i.e. first order differences), we apply this method to reach stationarity within our dataset. The stationarity of the resulting series is tested with the Augmented Dickey-Fuller test (not reported). The regression formula for our empirical analysis is as follow:

$$\triangle IXpayments_t = \alpha + \beta_i \triangle DXpayments_{it} + \sum_{w=1}^{7} \gamma_w weekday_{wt} \\ + \sum_{m=1}^{12} \delta_m month_{mt} + \sum_{y=2011}^{2013} \theta_y year_{yt} + \epsilon_t \tag{1}$$

where $\triangle IXpayments_t$ is the change of quantity of payments within the respective cryptocurrency i, $\triangle DXpayments_{it}$ the change of quantity of payments within the other cryptocurrencies, ϵ_t the error term and α the constant. As we are interested in seasonal effects dummy variables for each year ($year_{yt}$), month ($month_{mt}$) and weekday ($weekday_{wt}$) are included too.

4.3 Dataset

Cryptocurrencies rely on the concept of a blockchain which is stored on every client of the respective network. We exploit this mechanism to obtained our the dataset directly from the blockchain of the respective cryptocurrency, i.e. Bitcoin, Litecoin and Namecoin. In particular we calculate the Xpayments (transaction count) where X stands for the first letter of the respective cryptocurrency, e.g. Lpayments is the daily quantity of payments within Litecoin. As our analysis takes into account the exchange-rate between Bitcoin and USD (BTCUSD) we further rely on an exchange that offers trading of USD against Bitcoin and vice versa. We choose to use one of major exchanges operating during our observation timespan: Mt. Gox. These both sources are aggregated on a daily basis likewise found in other related studies.

As we want to analyze the interconnection of these three cryptocurrencies we choose the start of our observation timespan in the respect of the introduction dates of these three cryptocurrencies. As outlined in the Sect. 2.5 the cryptocurrency which was introduced most recently is Litecoin in October 2011, therefore our dataset begins on the 10th of October 2011. Regarding the end of the observation timespan we choose the 10th of October 2013 which results in a timespan of two years (i.e. 732 days).

5 Results and Discussion

5.1 Descriptive Results

The descriptive statistics of our dataset are presented in Table 1. By comparing the mean quantity of payments within these three cryptocurrencies it can be concluded that Bitcoin is clearing leading which shows the wide usage of this cryptocurrency. One attempt to explain this observation might be the age of Bitcoin. However, as Litecoin is the youngest cryptocurrency within our sample and exhibits more than twice as much payments compared to Namecoin this explanation is short-handed as the relation between Namecoin and Litecoin would then be the other way around. The same order (Bitcoin, Litecoin, Namecoin) is observed when comparing minimums and maximums leaving us to the conclusion that the underlying mechanism driving the quantity of payments is not depending on the age of the respective cryptocurrency. This observation is also shared by visually inspecting the chart (see Fig. 1) which shows the quantity of payments per day. The chart also shows that the quantity of payments heavily increases over time for Bitcoin and partly Litecoin as they start to increase. Interestingly, Namecoin – once again – does not follow this trend giving a first indication the quantity of payments differs along with the intended usage of the cryptocurrency. The correlations between our variables are shown in Table 2. Litecoin and Bitcoin share more commonalities between each other as correlations between quantity of payments in between these two cryptocurrencies and the Bitcoin exchange-rate also correlates with quantity of payments of Litecoin. Namecoin stands again apart by showing no correlation to other cryptocurrencies. This further supports the assumption that the intended usage of the respective cryptocurrency affects whether the quantity of payments relate to each other. But these effect may observed due to the trend in the timeseries therefore we further perform a regression analysis.

Table 1. Descriptive statistics of the dataset used.

Variable	N	Mean	Median	Std. Dev	Min	Max
Bpayments	732	32,140.010	33,542.500	19,667.200	4,674	72,187
Npayments	732	1,042.795	624.000	1,293.793	250	10,291
Lpayments	732	2,834.831	1,744.500	2,461.980	405	22,323
BTCUSD	732	39.698	11.915	49.347	2.290	237.567

Table 2. Correlations between our variables.

	Bpayments	Npayments	Lpayments	BTCUSD
Bpayments	1			
Npayments	-0.096	1		
Lpayments	0.508	0.017	1	
BTCUSD	0.697	-0.010	0.708	1

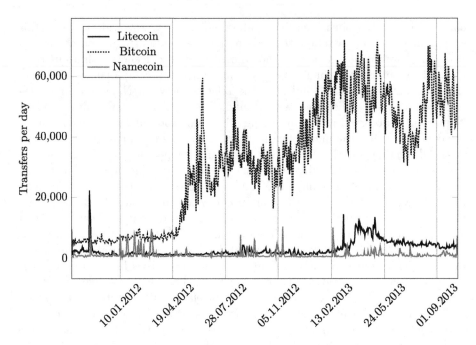

Fig. 1. Quantity of payments per day in Bitcoin, Litecoin & Namecoin.

5.2   Regression Results

Table 3 exhibit the detailed results of our regression analysis. We apply several multivariate regressions to answer our research questions. For each cryptocurrency we run two regressions: (i) a regression where we regress the quantity of payments against the seasonal parameters year, month and weekday as dummy variables. (ii) a regression where we regress the quantity of payments against the quantity of payments of the other two cryptocurrencies. To further analyze the connection of the most prominent cryptocurrency Bitcoin against the other two we include in the second regression the exchange-rate to account for a possible indirect effect via the exchange-rate. For additional robustness we also run a regression with all variables introduced, as significance levels shown in Table 3 stay the same and due to space limitations we omit these results within our paper. We report the coefficients along with the standard errors (in brackets), respective significance levels are reported as follow: $^*p{<}0.1$; $^{**}p{<}0.05$; $^{***}p{<}0.01$.

Research Question 1: Seasonalities Within Cryptocurrencies. The regressions devoted to the this research question are (2) for Bitcoin (4) for Litecoin and (6) for Namecoin. For the latter one we find no seasonal effects therefore validating the observations made in the previous section that Namecoin stands within these three cryptocurrencies aside. In the case of the other two cryptocurrencies only the weekday influences the quantity of payments. Consequently we conclude that the usage of cryptocurrencies do not follow monthly

Table 3. Regression results

	Dependent variable:					
	$\triangle Bpayments$		$\triangle Lpayments$		$\triangle Npayments$	
	(1)	(2)	(3)	(4)	(5)	(6)
$\triangle Bpayments$			0.002		0.003	
			(0.008)		(0.008)	
$\triangle Npayments$	0.061		0.028			
	(0.166)		(0.034)			
$\triangle Lpayments$	0.047				0.034	
	(0.183)				(0.041)	
$\triangle BTCUSD$	74.568**		4.792		4.363	
	(37.197)		(7.562)		(8.343)	
February		−335.550		−8.990		−0.212
		(986.790)		(205.067)		(227.783)
March		−541.679		91.144		−1.281
		(966.226)		(200.794)		(223.036)
April		−404.500		−78.830		17.221
		(973.848)		(202.378)		(224.795)
May		−96.372		−48.245		−5.373
		(965.926)		(200.732)		(222.967)
June		−752.967		−20.548		1.935
		(974.156)		(202.442)		(224.866)
July		−124.682		−17.892		−15.125
		(965.777)		(200.700)		(222.932)
August		−192.301		4.527		−3.694
		(966.151)		(200.778)		(223.019)
September		−608.334		−71.206		7.710
		(974.002)		(202.410)		(224.831)
October		−426.422		−76.042		137.688
		(1,017.887)		(211.530)		(234.961)
November		−138.067		−3.707		39.506
		(1,073.898)		(223.170)		(247.890)
December		−411.871		26.010		37.550
		(1,066.823)		(221.699)		(246.257)
Year 2012		59.638		103.637		42.223
		(804.923)		(167.273)		(185.802)
Year 2013		93.299		113.205		82.062
		(905.387)		(188.151)		(208.992)
Monday		3,398.175***		−149.262		−5.554
		(744.577)		(154.732)		(171.872)
Tuesday		2,885.071***		−34.706		−67.901
		(744.520)		(154.721)		(171.859)
Wednesday		2,909.034***		179.465		−196.888
		(744.291)		(154.673)		(171.806)
Thursday		2,205.882***		258.422*		202.712
		(745.745)		(154.975)		(172.142)
Saturday		1,266.716*		311.917**		23.079
		(745.805)		(154.988)		(172.156)
Sunday		4,997.591***		26.661		10.122
		(746.053)		(155.039)		(172.213)
Constant	56.834	−2,185.864*	−9.731	−171.548	8.677	−56.242
	(203.809)	(1,180.680)	(41.330)	(245.360)	(45.594)	(272.539)
Observations	731	731	731	731	731	731
R²	0.006	0.073	0.002	0.022	0.002	0.009
Residual Std. Error	5,506.884 (df = 727)	5,376.800 (df = 711)	1,116.702 (df = 727)	1,117.367 (df = 711)	1,231.907 (df = 727)	1,241.138 (df = 711)
F Statistic	1.429 (df = 3; 727)	2.953*** (df = 19; 711)	0.400 (df = 3; 727)	0.860 (df = 19; 711)	0.382 (df = 3; 727)	0.334 (df = 19; 711)

and yearly patterns like number of trades in securities trading (e.g. as shown by [29]). Further we observe small similarities between Bitcoin and Litecoin, i.e. that the quantity of payments is significant positive for two weekdays (i.e. Thursday and Saturday). Most interestingly this effect is strongest for Bitcoin where six weekdays are significant. The coefficients are extraordinary high for Sunday and Monday. As we use coordinated universal time (UTC) for our aggregation, the high coefficient might also caused by volume caused on a Sunday. This is an indication that most activity in Bitcoin happens on the weekend thus we can conclude that Bitcoin is used during free time on the weekend mostly neglecting the assumption that Bitcoin is for businesses (b2b) purposes within our observation timespan. Further we add to the results of [23, 24] as we are able to map the aggregated behavior of user patterns passively.

Research Question 2: Connection Between Cryptocurrencies. The results relevant for second research question are the models (1) for Bitcoin, (3) for Litecoin and (5) for Namecoin. Regarding the connection between these cryptocurrencies we observe that sharing the same technical basis does not translate into the same payment behavior patterns. Even indirect effects, which we address by including the exchange-rate of Bitcoin against the USD, do indicate that a connection between these three cryptocurrencies could not be made. Therefore we conclude that the user groups which are attracted and using these cryptocurrencies are different, at least measured by their payment behavior.

6   Conclusion

Cryptocurrencies exist because there exist an increasing money demand for this form of money. The market development of cryptocurrencies illustrates an institutional change how payments can be released without the need of a trusted central party to clear virtual transactions within today's digital market economy. Payments can be organized free of bureaucratic involvement to compensate a lack of trust. This developments remain just in the beginning, and yet are gaining momentum in reducing transaction costs. This might has contributed to the fact that cryptocurrencies have gained within the last years an increasing importance resulting in increased activity within these Bitcoin descendants (i.e. Altcoins).

These cryptocurrencies allow researchers to observe every transaction being made offering an unique possibility to analyze many aspects of payment patterns and payment behavior, as well for future research in this field. We address in this work the question how seasonalities affect payment pattern and payment behavior within the two oldest descendants of Bitcoin: Litecoin & Namecoin. We find that weekdays have a significant influence on the quantity of payments for Bitcoin and Litecoin. Namecoin clearly deviates from this pattern as no effect could found-was evident. This gives an indication that the intended usage of each demanded coin, be it Litecoin, Namecoin or any other for the cryptocurrency, payment system in the case of Bitcoin and Litecoin and a decentral name system in the case Namecoin, has an influence on the seasonality and thus user behavior. One might expect that alternative cryptocurrencies to Bitcoin (i.e. Altcoins) exhibit only an extend/mutation of the already established Bitcoin cryptocurrency, because they share a similar technical design. Our analysis illustrated that the identical technical basis does not necessarily fosters identical payment behavior of users, but quite the opposite. Our results stay the same even when taking into account the price in terms of the USD exchange-rate of Bitcoin. This further supports the assumption that the intended usage of the respective cryptocurrency affects whether the quantity of payments relate to each other. Therefore we conclude that the user groups who demand money are attracted and using these cryptocurrencies differently. In short, we argue that utility to demand money, for example of Namecoins, differs among Altcoins, at least measured by their payment behavior. Thus, our analysis showed that Altcoins do not represents just a replicate, which is substitutable over time and payment patterns and payment behavior might not converge but diverge further in the near future.

We contribute to the body of knowledge in several ways: (i) we show that the activity in a payment system is influenced by seasonal effects, in our case weekdays. Therefore we add to the literature stream which analyzes seasonal effects in financial markets, e.g. [28, 29, 32]. (ii) We show that sharing same technological does not translates to the same payment behavior. (iii) That aggregated user behavior within cryptocurrencies can be mapped passively extending the previous work (e.g. [24, 27]) on anonymity within Bitcoin with other cryptocurrencies. Still it is important to note that we also face limitations within our analysis. As we want to ensure that each cryptocurrency selected exists long enough to attract a significant number of users we choose theselected to three oldest cryptocurrencies, therefore our results might be dependent on the cryptocurrencies solely. Our research gives a first indication and further research should take different cryptocurrencies (e.g. Peercoin, Dogecoin or Ripple) into account. Another limitation is that we only analyze daily aggregated data, therefore we are not able to observe intraday payment patterns. Within further research we want focus us on intra-day payment patterns and the analysis of payment volumes.

We conclude on this findings in our work that payment patterns and payment behaviors on the basis of cryptocurrencies will continue to diverge.

References

1. Nakamoto, S.: Bitcoin: A peer-to-peer electronic cash system. Working Paper (2008)
2. Coinmarketcap: Crypto-Currency Market Capitalizations. https://coinmarketcap.com/
3. Business Insider: This Is Litecoin, The 'Silver' to Bitcoin's 'Gold'. https://coinmarketcap.com/
4. Forbes: Bitcoin? Yawn. CheapAir Is Now Taking Litecoin and Dogecoin. http://www.forbes.com/sites/erikamorphy/2014/09/03/bitcoin-yawn-cheapair-is-now-taking-litecoin-and-dogecoin/
5. Coindesk: Altcoin News - Daily Cryptocurrency Articles. http://www.coindesk.com/technology/altcoins/)
6. Weber, M.: The Protestant Ethic and the Spirit of Capitalism: Translated from the German by Talcott Parsons. Charles Scribner's Sons, New York (1930)
7. Luhmann, N.: Die Wirtschaft der Gesellschaft. Suhrkamp, Frankfurt (1988)
8. Quintata Diaz, J.M.: Money and freedom in the view of polanyi's great transformation: decommodification by constituting alternative monetary institutions?. In: Fourth International Conference on Degrowth for Ecological Sustainability and Social Equity (2014)
9. Quintata Diaz, J.M.: The Merger of Cryptography and Economics: Do cryptographic economic systems lead to the future of Money and Payments? Working Discussion Paper (2014)
10. Schricker, W., Rubine, E.: Geld, Kredit und Waehrung. Verlag fuer Wirtschaftsskripte, Muenchen (1992)
11. Vaubel, R.: Real exchange rate changes in the european community: a new approach to the determination of optimum currency areas. J. Int. Econ. 8(2), 319–339 (1978)

12. Swanson, T.: Great Number of Chains: A Guide to Smart Contracts, Smart Property and Trustless Asset Management. Amazon Digital Services, Seattle (2014)
13. Luther, W.J.: Crypto-currencies, Network Effects, and Switching Costs. Working Paper (2013)
14. Dowd, K., Greenaway, D.: Currency competition, network externalities and switching costs: Towards an alternative view of optimum currency areas. Econ. J. **103**(420), 1180–1189 (1993)
15. Gandal, N., Halaburda, H.: Competition in the Crypto-currency Market. Working Paper (2014)
16. Courtois, N.T.: On The Longest Chain Rule and Programmed Self-Destruction of Crypto Currencies. Working Paper (2014)
17. Kaplanov, N.: Nerdy money: Bitcoin, the private digital currency, and the case against its regulation. Working Paper (2012)
18. Yermack, D.: Is Bitcoin a Real Currency?. National Bureau of Economic Research, Working Paper No. 19747 (2013)
19. Glaser, F., Zimmermann, K., Haferkorn, M., Weber, M.C., Siering, M.: Bitcoin-Asset or currency? revealing users' hidden intentions. In: Proceedings of the 22th European Conference on Information Systems (2014)
20. Glaser, F., Haferkorn, M., Weber, M.C., Zimmermann, K.: How to price a digital currency? empirical insights on the influence of media coverage on the bitcoin bubble. Bank. Inf. Technol. **15**(1), 21–32 (2014)
21. Kristoufek, L.: Bitcoin meets google trends and wikipedia: quantifying the relationship between phenomena of the internet era. Sci. Rep. **3**(3415), 1–7 (2013)
22. Buchholz, M., Delaney, J., Warren, J.: Bits and Bets - Information, Price Volatility, and Demand for Bitcoin. Working Paper (2012)
23. Androulaki, E., Karame, G.O., Roeschlin, M., Scherer, T., Capkun, S.: Evaluating user privacy in bitcoin. In: Sadeghi, A.-R. (ed.) FC 2013. LNCS, vol. 7859, pp. 34–51. Springer, Heidelberg (2013)
24. Reid, F., Harrigan, M.: An analysis of anonymity in the bitcoin system. In: Altshuler, Y., Elovici, Y., Cremers, A.B., Aharony, N., Pentland, A. (eds.) Security and Privacy in Social Networks, pp. 197–223. Springer, New York (2013)
25. Karame, G.O., Androulaki, E., Capkun, S.: Double-spending fast payments in bitcoin. In: Proceedings of the 2012 ACM Conferenceon Computer and Communications Security, pp. 906–917 (2012)
26. Ron, D., Shamir, A.: Quantitative analysis of the full bitcoin transaction graph. In: Sadeghi, A.-R. (ed.) FC 2013. LNCS, vol. 7859, pp. 6–24. Springer, Heidelberg (2013)
27. Ober, M., Katzenbeisser, S., Hamacher, K.: Structure and anonymity of the bitcoin transaction graph. Future Internet **5**(2), 237–250 (2013)
28. Harris, L.: A transaction data study of weekly and intradaily patterns in stock returns. J. Financ. Econ. **16**(1), 99–117 (1986)
29. Chordia, T., Roll, R., Subrahmanyam, A.: Market liquidity and trading activity. J. Finance **56**(2), 501–530 (2001)
30. Hasbrouck, J., Seppi, D.J.: Common factors in prices, order flows, and liquidity. J. Financ. Econ. **59**(3), 383–441 (2001)
31. Hillard, J.E., Tucker, A.L.: A note on weekday, intraday, and overnight patterns in the interbank foreign exchange and listed currency options markets. J. Bank. Finance **16**(1), 1159–1171 (1992)
32. Hong, H., Yu, J.: Gone fishin': Seasonality in trading activity and asset prices. J. Finan. Markets **12**(4), 672–702 (2009)

Survey of Financial Market Visualization Utilizing Interactive Media Technology

Artur Lugmayr[(✉)]

School of Media, Creative Arts, and Media,
Visualisation and Interactive Media (VisMedia),
Curtin University, Perth, Australia
lartur@acm.org
http://www.artur-lugmayr.com

Abstract. Big Data, as well as the visualization of data is a buzzword today. This publication surveys latest trends in visualization in financial industries. A very basic framework considering the different data, interaction, user, method, and evaluation methods is presented. Following a basic review of the existing literature in financial industry visualization, the framework is described in further depths, and shades insight into the different criteria of financial visualization in e.g. the contexts of regulation, market observation, prediction of market forecasting, and visualization of statistical information. The publication rounds up with a discussion of latest trends in media technology, and how these might impact the way how financial industries adopt these into their work-practices, such as virtual currencies, crowd-funding, social media trading, crowd-sourcing, or analysis of financial news. Thus, this publication manifested as a survey article about latest interactive media technology, and how this technology is enriching financial industries in many aspects for the purpose of visualization.

Keywords: Visualisation · Financial industries · Stock returns · Information visualization · Media technology · Trading · Investment · Data analytics · Big data · Sentiment analysis · Business information

1 Introduction

The prime goal of information visualization is to related to "human activity of forming a mental model of something", thus to "amplify cognitive performance, [and] not just creating interesting pictures" (Spence 2001). As important note, "visualization can be enhanced with computer support, but has nothing to do with computers per se" (Card 2012). Financial visualization can be considered as a use-case of information visualization in a very particular domain with specific use requirements. It includes several activities of forming a mental model of financial news, tick data, data on corporate level, knowledge and information visualization, data presentation, or the envisioning of financial risk. In particular the support through new advancements in interactive media technology, as computer graphics, multimedia presentation, audio/video content analysis, or interactivity allows to enhance representation and presentation of financial information and knowledge and intensify the cognitive experience of the system users. Also the integration of more advanced phenomenon in digital media, such as the

© Springer International Publishing Switzerland 2015
A. Lugmayr (Ed.): FinanceCom 2014, LNBIP 217, pp. 121–134, 2015.
DOI: 10.1007/978-3-319-28151-3_9

application of social media in trading, or investor based crowdfunding enables new possibilities in the world of finances far beyond visualization techniques. Within the scope of this paper, the possibilities of new interactive media technologies in the context of financial industries are investigated and their potential demonstrated. A framework for advanced financial visualizations is presented, and key parameters are presented.

In particular recent trends cause a lot of confusion on financial markets: bitcoins, crowd-investing, crowdsourcing, disruptive change, new models for customer relationship management, financial crisis, virtual currencies (example games, amazon, bitcoin). These let new indicators as e.g. the LUGO indicator based on sentiment aggregation emerge (Lugmayr and Gossen 2012).

The research paper is written based on a survey of available literature in the domain of financial market visualizations, and discussing these sources with the latest trends that interactive media technologies gave birth to. It is more of the type of a basic introduction work, rather than a full investigation, however, it will briefly give an overview of the current trends, methods, and techniques. The work concludes by the development of a basic framework, which can be utilized in realizing visualizations in this domain.

2   Application Areas and Related Works

Financial industry is a rather niche domain in scientific research, and literature is very scares as the scientific and research community is rather small. However, within the scope of this section, a few example works that deal with financial visualization are presented. Before considering very specialized literature, it's essential to understand the background of visualization and envisioning information. There exists a wide range of literature, but (Liu et al. 2014) provides an excellent survey of recent advances. A very basic work on historical and visual aspects on information visualization can be found in (Tufte 1990). A more modern and comprehensive overview can be found in (Spence 2014). The reference provides an excellent overview of information visualization across domains. Within the scope of this publication, we extended the taxonomy of visualization techniques from this work. An excellent review of existing studies related to methods applied in visualization evaluation from a consumer viewpoint has been conducted by (Lam et al. 2012). Some works relate to challenges, publishing results of their entries, as e.g. the Australasian eResearch Forum (Anon 2009). An excellent work, reviewing sentiment analysis using social media can be found in (Lugmayr 2013).

Visualization in financial markets have a wide range of application areas in financial industries. Speaking in terms of the visualization process, particular techniques, methods, and interaction capabilities have to be contextualized to the application context. In the following, a set of basic scenarios are presented on the basis of the discussions in (Lugmayr 2013), which based their work on (Lombardi et al. 2011):

- Marketing, customer management, and promotion
- Market surveillance, monitoring and analysis

- Investor support, management, and data analysis
- Technical indicators supporting investment decisions

Table 1 gives a brief overview of research work that has been conducted in the field of visualization, and relates these to the application scenarios mentioned above.

Table 1. Overview of scenarios of financial visualization

Research type	Application areas	Example references
Marketing, consumer management, and promotion		
Visualization Technique	Overview of tools for financial data visualization	(Sylvester 2008)
Market surveillance, monitoring, and analysis		
Visual analytics	Regulation of electronic order book markets	(Paddrik et al. 2014)
Financial news analytics	Trend visualization of financial news	(Ng and Qu 2014)
Technical indicators supporting investment decision making		
Media visualizations	Sentiment analysis with social media data	(Lugmayr 2013)
Visualization techniques	Sunburst visualizations	(Ramsay 2015)
Investment support, management, and data analysis		
Market analysis	Market analysis and forecasting to support trading	(Dwyer and Eades 2002)
Technical indicators	Statistical modeling and visualization of financial data	(Tsay 2014)
Text analysis and mining	Text mining & sentiment analysis	(Nassirtoussi et al. 2014)
Interaction Models	Gesture based interaction	(Shenoy 2015)
General overviews of information visualization		
Validation and evaluation of methods	Overview of empirical user-centered visualization evaluations	(Lam et al. 2012)
Art of information visualization	Envisioning information	(Tufte 1990)

3   Information Visualization in the Financial Domain

Information visualization on general level deals with the "progress of methods for enhancing density, complexity, dimensionality, and beauty of data" (Tufte 1990). Within the scope of this section of the research work, a first taxonomy for information visualization in the financial domain is developed, and principle application areas are presented.

3.1   Framework for Visualization in Finance Industry

A basic framework for visualization in financial industry has to cover a wide range of aspects. The framework needs to include the basic characteristics of underlying data as e.g. time-series data, as well as data on corporate level e.g. for equities. It also has to consider existing techniques that are typically used in visualizations, as e.g. box plots or point representations. The framework requires also an inclusion of interaction models, who the end-user can interact with the actual visualization, as well as verification and evaluation models to evaluate the visualization from various angles.

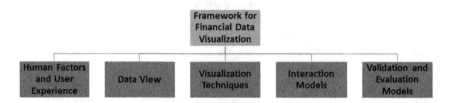

Fig. 1. Basic components of a financial industry visualization

Figure 1 depicts the top level requirements for the components of a framework in finance industry. It consists of the following major components:

- **Human Factors and User Experience:** this dimension deals with several aspects of human factors including content coding, perception, and end-user experience;
- **Data View:** visualization underlying aspects of data are related to this dimension, and include data analytics, information density, data dimensions, or data types;
- **Visualization Techniques:** set of techniques utilized for visualization ranging from simple; time-varying; relation, networks, and connection; hierarchies; to advanced techniques;
- **Validation and Evaluation Models:** tools, techniques, and methods for valuation and evaluation of human factors including user-experience, data, visualization technique, and interaction models;
- **Interaction Models:** wide range of interaction models such as WIMP, post-WIMP, multi-modality, up to more advanced interaction techniques utilized in virtual or augmented reality environments or ubiquitous media;

3.2   Financial Data, Its Characteristics and It's Analysis

In particular in times of algorithmic and automated trading, the importance of methods in designing financial systems gains importance, as the source data characteristics copes with most definitions of BigData – thus we deal with data following the 4Vs. Nevertheless, the data characteristics extends towards increasing unstructuredness, real-time constraints and availability, multi-facededness, and increasing complexity. The data contains a rather high amount of knowledge that requires extraction from the available data sources. Thus financial data is a prime example for the simply categorization of data in structured, semi-structured, and unstructured data (Spence 2014) in the domain of information design. However, the available data allows a much more granular categorization, which is discussed in a later stage of this chapter.

The prime data source in financial information systems is structured data, thus data with a very particular presentation and representation as e.g. database entries of time-series data of stock quotes. Semi-structured data is available through metadata languages such used for business applications, and it's usage is – but not limited to – in business information system, data exchange, or news broadcasting through RSS feeds. However, the main challenge (as is also outside the financial industry) is the processing of unstructured data, such as textual data e.g. for sentiment analysis (Lugmayr and Gossen 2012).

Financial data, as any other form of data, can either be *nominal* (e.g. market state – bearish/bullish), *ordinal* (e.g. ranking of returns – asset B brings a larger return than asset F, and asset A brings larger returns than asset C), *categorical* (e.g. asset type – index-certificate, shares, commodities), *relationships* (e.g. relationship between currency value and asset prices), *abstract* (e.g. graph representation of money flow of worldwide investors' returns), *complex* (e.g. text, audio, video, images, media), *composites* (e.g. combination of asset type and market state), *metadata* (e.g. meta information about single financial assets), or completely *unstructured* (e.g. shareholder meeting brief).

Despite this wide range of data types, time-series and volume pricing can be considered as the major data types and are most wide spread in financial industry. We also can view the corporate context, thus viewing financial industries from an information system perspective, which allows another classification of data. In this classification, we consider a business information systems view, where data is categorized according the organizational level inside the organization, as e.g. discussed in (Luadon and Laudon 2003).

3.3   Information Visualization Process

Figure 2 illustrates the visualization process as defined in (Spence 2014). However, the figure extends the idea of (Spence 2014) by three aspects as essential parts of the

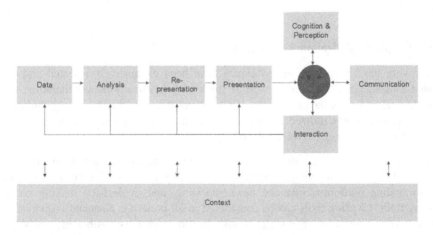

Fig. 2. Visualization process extended from (Spence 2014) by the essential components of interaction, contextually, and communication, which were not stated in the source.

information visualization process: *context*, *interactivity*, and *communication*. Besides the other components of the visualization process as e.g. data, analysis, data representation, data presentation, and cognition & perception, the newly introduced components play an essential role in the overall visualization process, as e.g. visualization are getting increasingly interactive; either virtual or face-to-face communication can be considered as an important part of the visualization process; and the context and in particular the requirements for the application play a considerable role in designing visualizations.

4 Visualization Techniques: Representation and Presentation of Data

Figure 3 gives an overview of potential visualization techniques in financial industry. In principle we can distinguish between:

- Simple visualization techniques for data re-presentations
- Time varying visualizations
- Visualization of relationships, networks, and connections
- Visualization of hierarchical information
- Advanced visualizations and data presentations

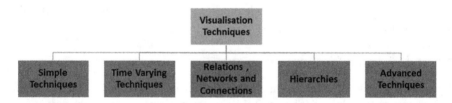

Fig. 3. Basic categories of visualization techniques to be applied in financial markets visualizations.

4.1 Simple Visualization Techniques

These very basic visualization techniques have been exhaustively research and presented across scientific works, as well as stock trading strategy related literature. One excellent reference for the exploration of various tools as e.g. charting, dashboards, and a few advanced tools utilized for time-series data supporting market forecasting and decision making is e.g. (Sylvester 2008).

Charting: The most commonly used visualization technique in financial industries is charting. Charting, chart analysis, and real-time display of time-series data is all-present across trading platforms, financial news reporting, and in decision making on the trading floor. Charting tools can be considered as all-present in financial visualization. These tools combine a large scale of visualization techniques either in stand-alone fashion, or as a combination of these: quote charts, tables, or candle stick charts.

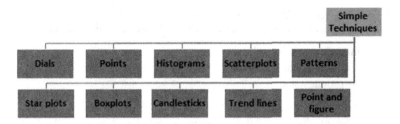

Fig. 4. Simple visualization techniques (partially based on (Spence 2014)).

The underlying data can be characterized as structured numerical time-series data consisting of a sequence of stock quotes, volume, and time information (Fig. 4).

Dashboards: Dashboards utilize dials or hemispherical items to display "the relative placement of data [...] between two extremes" (Sylvester 2008). This simple technique allows a user-friendly, and fast perceptible understanding of the displayed information. In combination with other techniques, these set of tools provides a powerful visualization method.

Information Displays: Information displays are another commonly used visualization techniques in financial industries and combine multiple visualizations into one canvas. Information displays can combine different simple visualization techniques in the context of trading to support buying or selling decisions. Examples are e.g. equity information overviews, active trading positions, news tickers, or combinations of various charts under one display are. The underlying data can be also characterised as mostly structured numerical time-series data, numerical data expressing equity information, trend information, ordinal information as e.g. ranking of equities, or categorical information as equity type.

4.2   Time Varying Visualization Techniques

Time varying visualization techniques are illustrated in Fig. 5. There are two possible techniques available: theme rivers, and arc diagrams.

Fig. 5. Time Varying Techniques (Spence 2014)).

4.3   Visualizations of Relations, Networks, and Connections

A more complex type of visualization is required for depicting relations, networks, and connections. The use in financial industries is rather wide – observation of links between markets, regulatory market observation, and identification of relations between market participants. In principle we can distinguish between the following types:

- data and inter-data relationships
- networks, intra-personal and social
- information propagation
- market dependencies

An overview of the potential visualization techniques that can be utilized for visualizing this type is depicted in Fig. 6. One prime example for this type of visualization is the visualization of market conduct for regulatory authorities, e.g. by order tracing graphs to understand market evolution over time (see e.g. (Paddrik et al. 2014)).

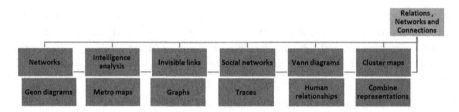

Fig. 6. Visualization techniques for relations, networks, and connections (partially based on (Spence 2014)).

Visualization of relations, networks, and connections also relates to data visualizing the causalities between market data, such as e.g. sentiment and stock market returns as e.g. illustrated in (Sheu et al. 2009) and in (Zouaoui et al. 2010). Nevertheless, this type of visualization focuses on the visualization of inter-data relationships, but can be extended towards models focusing on stock exchange networks, online communities, or stock exchange structures, as e.g. discussed in (Sakalyte 2009). Other research works focus e.g. on models for news propagation, especially how these is happening the world of online communities (Garg et al. 2011).

4.4 Visualization of Hierarchical Information

The visualization of hierarchical data information is another category that requires consideration when talking about visualization in financial industries. One very typical visualization technique that is commonly used are tree-maps (see e.g. (Sylvester 2008) or the patented sunburst display (Ramsay 2015). These techniques are illustrated in Fig. 7.

Fig. 7. Visualization techniques for relations, networks, and connections (partially based on (Spence 2014)).

4.5   Advanced Techniques in Information Visualization

There exist many advanced techniques for information visualization techniques in the financial domain, as e.g. the typically used heatmaps, textual visualizations, or more complex media based visualizations. Examples for these kind of visualizations are all present in financial market industries. Applications range from semantic data network visualizations, where e.g. ontologies are utilized to describe market knowledge (Lombardi et al. 2011) or financial decision support applications allow to apply a very wide set of advanced application scenarios. Many of the visualization techniques that can be utilized within this scope are depicted in Fig. 8.

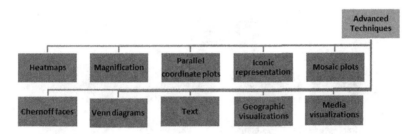

Fig. 8. Advanced visualization techniques (partially based on (Spence 2014)).

Especially text based visualizations gain on importance, as the sheer volume of unstructured data is increasing. This includes the application of textual analysis techniques on text corpora, with data sources from financial news, social media, investment reports, or any other sources. Geographic visualizations that tie the visualization to location are another advanced technique which is wide spread in financial market industries. These include e.g. the utilization of heatmaps or financial weather charts of the global financial market climate.

Nevertheless, we should not neglect the use of more advanced media technologies in financial market industries. These include the application of virtual reality, augmented reality, or 3D technology to allow more insights into data. The emergence of these new technologies, enriched financial visualizations by e.g. gesture based interaction (Shenoy 2015). Especially the world of ubiquitous media (or ambient media) (Lugmayr 2007; Lugmayr 2006; Lugmayr et al. 2013) enable location based services, news delegation via mobiles, personalization capabilities (Lugmayr et al. 2008; Lugmayr et al. 2013), or even more advanced context sensitive applications. Thus a visualization becomes a matter of being part of the real world. The use in financial industries is manifold as e.g. increased mobility of traders, interaction with novel in-air screens (Rakkolainen and Lugmayr 2007), or collection of market intelligence.

We can extend the notion of advanced visualizations even towards new structures of narrative and storytelling. In particular the analysis of financial news requires background knowledge of story structure, as well as allow insights how 'serious' stories – serious storytelling - about market facts can be told to increase a quick and fast perception of news of traders or other market participants.

5   Human Factors and User Experience

Another component of the framework are human factors and user-experience, which are an essential part when talking about information and data visualization. Figure 9 illustrated the different aspects: content coding, perception, cognition, and experience. Several of these components deal with particular aspects, as e.g. the content presentation to the user, how the user perceive the presented visualization and cognitive aspects. The knowledge creation process can be described by user-experience factors. However, to describe these components in further depth would be beyond the scope of this publication.

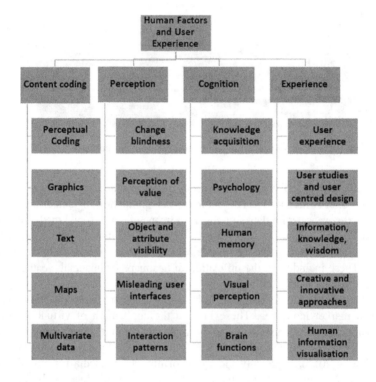

Fig. 9. Human factors and user experience in visualization frameworks

6   Interactivity and Collaborative Techniques

A very active research community is investigation human-computer-interaction methods in recent years. The increasing amount of applications requiring customer experience, new interaction models, and more collaborative types of applications is one of these trends. However, within the scope of this publication, we can consider, that the framework for financial markets visualizations can consist of the following components (Fig. 10):

- application and service interactivity
- communication capabilities
- inter-device/inter-person collaboration
- crowd and grassroots phenomenon

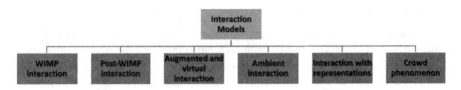

Fig. 10. Interaction models for financial market visualizations.

Nevertheless, to avoid focusing on the first three types of interactivity and collaboration techniques, we would like to shade more light on crowd phenomenon that have been emerging during recent years. Most recent media technology introduced many new successful facets in our daily life, and they will not stop in being applied in financial markets. In particular the phenomenon of the crowd based on new collaborative media technology found already its way into financial markets, and might disrupt existing business models. These include:

- crowd sourcing for innovations, labor, concepts, ideas, and new products
- crowd financial markets as e.g. through equities, currencies, or funding
- crowd knowledge as e.g. knowledge and expertise sharing
- crowd community as e.g. self-help or experience sharing

A few recent case studies focus on these phenomena, and shade light on the basic principles (Lasrado and Lugmayr 2013; Lasrado and Lugmayr 2014). Visualization techniques in this domain have been very poorly researched and require a more thorough investigation in the future.

7 Validation and Evaluation Models

A framework for visualization in financial industry has to include methods for validation and evaluation of visualizations, including several aspects as e.g. user-experience, quality, processes, and common practices. Common techniques normally utilized in the field of information visualization, can be adopted for the use in financial industries as well. An excellent review of techniques has been provided in (Lam et al. 2012), which provides a categorization of methods based on an investigation of submissions to information visualization conferences. (Lam et al. 2012) distinguishes between methods for *data analysis evaluation*, and *understanding information visualizations*, and clustered various techniques as follows:

- criteria for data analysis evaluation
  - environments and work practices
  - visual data analysis and reasoning
  - communication through visualization
  - collaborative data analysis
- evaluation methods to understand information visualization
  - user-performance
  - user-experience
  - visualization algorithms

In the context of financial industries, we can refine these clusters, and link these to the particular requirements that are commonly emerging from the type of applications that are utilized there. Thus, viewing it from the information visualization process point of view, the context of the particular application would be pre-dominant which are enlisted in Table 1.

8   Conclusion and Future Work

This research work represents a survey of visualization techniques in the financial domain. It presented a basic framework for the utilization of latest interactive media technology in the domain, and was shading light on the different characteristics, aspects, and features. The paper also investigated more modern approaches for applying latest digital media technology, as e.g. crowd based phenomenon and virtual and augmented modes of visualization. Nevertheless, much future work is required in the experimentation how modern interactive media technology can support financial industries in knowledge mining, decision making, risk visualization, among many other application scenarios.

References

Anon: Visualization Challange (2009). http://www.eresearch.edu.au/viswinners2009

Card, S.: Human Computer Interaction Handbook: Fundamentals, Evolving Technologies, and Emerging Applications. In: Jacko, J.A. (ed.), pp. 515–548. CRC press, Boca Raton (2012)

Dwyer, T., Eades, P.: Visualising a fund manager flow graph with columns and worms. In: 2002 Proceedings of the Sixth International Conference on Information Visualisation, pp. 147–152 (2002)

Garg, R., Smith, M.D., Telang, R.: Measuring information diffusion in an online community. J. Manag. Inf. Syst. **28**(2), 11–38 (2011)

Lam, H., et al.: Empirical studies in information visualization: seven scenarios. IEEE Trans. Visual. Comput. Graphics **18**(9), 1520–1536 (2012)

Lasrado, L., Lugmayr, A.: Crowdfunding in Finland - A new alternative disruptive funding instrument for businesses. In: Lugmayr, A., et al., (eds.) Proceedings of the 17th International Academic MindTrek Conference. Association for Computer Machinery (ACM), Tampere, Finland (2013)

Lasrado, L.A., Lugmayr, A.: Equity crowdfunding -A finnish case study. In: 2014 IEEE International Conference on Multimedia and Expo Workshops (ICMEW), pp. 1–6 (2014)

Liu, S., et al.: A survey on information visualization: recent advances and challenges. Vis. Comput. **30**(12), 1373–1393 (2014). http://dx.doi.org/10.1007/s00371-013-0892-3

Lombardi, P., et al.: Definition of market surveillance, risk management, and retail brokerage usecases. In: FIRST - Large Scale Information Extraction and Integration Infrastructure for Supporting Financial Decission Making (IST STREP) (2011)

Luadon, K., Laudon, J.: Essentials of Management Information Systems. Prentice Hall - Pearson Educational International, New Jersey (2003)

Lugmayr, A., Reymann, S., Kemper, S., Dorsch, T., Roman, P.: Bits of personality everywhere: implicit user-generated content in the age of ambient media. In: International Symposium on Parallel and Distributed Processing with Applications, ISPA 2008, pp. 516–521 (2008)

Lugmayr, A., Serral, E., Scherp, A., Pogorelc, B., Mustaquim, M.: Ambient media today and tomorrow. Multimedia Tools Appl., 1–31 (2013)

Lugmayr, A.: Ambient media. Novatica **33**, 35–39 (2007)

Lugmayr, A.: The future is ambient. In: Proceedings of SPIE, vol. 6074, 607403 Multimedia on Mobile Devices II (2006)

Lugmayr, A., Zou, Y., Stockleben, B., Lindfors, K., Melakoski, C.: Categorization of ambient media projects on their business models, innovativeness, and characteristics–evaluation of Nokia Ubimedia MindTrek Award Projects of 2010. Multimedia Tools Appl. **66**, 33–57 (2013). http://dx.doi.org/10.1007/s11042-012-1143-8

Lugmayr, A.: Predicting the future of investor sentiment with social media in stock exchange investments: A basic framework for the DAX performance index. In: Friedrichsen, M., Muehl-Benninghaus, W. (eds.) Handbook of Social Media Management. Media Business and Innovation, pp. 565–589. Springer, Heidelberg (2013). http://dx.doi.org/10.1007/978-3-642-28897-5_33

Lugmayr, A., Gossen, G.: Evaluation of methods and techniques for language based sentiment analysis for DAX30 stock exchange - A first concept of a "LUGO" sentiment indicator. In: Lugmayr, A., et al. (eds.) Proceedings of the 5th International Workshop on Semantic Ambient Media Experience (SAME) - in Conjunction with Pervasive 2012. Tampere University of Technology (TUT), Newcastle, UK (2012)

Nassirtoussi, A.K., et al.: Text mining for market prediction: A systematic review. Expert Systems with Applications **41**(16), 7653–7670 (2014). http://www.sciencedirect.com/science/article/pii/S0957417414003455

Ng, Y.-W., Qu, H.: TrendFocus: Visualization of trends in financial news with indicator sets. In: 2014 International Conference on Big Data and Smart Computing (BIGCOMP), pp. 7–12 (2014)

Paddrik, M., et al.: The Role of Visual Analytics in the Regulation of Electronic Order Markets, Office of Financial Research (OFR) (2014). http://financialresearch.gov/staff-discussion-papers/files/OFRsdp2014-02_PaddrikHaynesToddBelingScherer_RoleofVisualAnalysisin RegulationofElectronicOrderBookMarkets.pdf

Rakkolainen, I., Lugmayr, A.: Immaterial display for interactive advertisements. In: ACM Conference on Advances in Computer Entertainment Technology, Salzburg, Austria, pp. 95–98 (2007)

Ramsay, N., Wampler, T.: Visualization and interaction with financial data using sunburst visualization (9021397) (2015). http://www.freepatentsonline.com/9021397.html

Sakalyte, J.: European stock exchange networks: connections, structure and complexity. Appl. Econ. Syst. Res. **3**(2), 31–39 (2009)

Shenoy, M.U., Kakkar, S.R., Sreepathy, A., Madhani, S.H.: 2015. Gesture-Based Visualization of Financial Data., (20150058774) (2015). http://www.freepatentsonline.com/y2015/0058774.html

Sheu, H.-J., Lu, Y.-C., Wei, Y.-C.: Causalities between the sentiment indicators and stock market returns under different market scenarios. Int. J. Bus. Finance Res. 4(1), 159–172 (2009)

Spence, R.: Information Visualization. Springer, Heidelberg (2001)

Spence, R.: Information Visualization: An Introduction. Springer, Switzerland (2014). https://books.google.com.au/books?id=uOosBQAAQBAJ

Sylvester, B.: The Visualization of Financial Data: A Review of Information Visualization Tools in the Financial data domain (2008). http://www.docme.ru/doc/834026/the-visualization-of-financial-data

Tsay, R.: An Introduction to Analysis of Financial Data with R. Wiley, Hoboken (2014)

Tufte, E.R.: Envisioning information. Graphics Press, Cheshire (1990). https://books.google.com.au/books?id=fW9jAAAAMAAJ

Zouaoui, M., Nouyrigat, G., Beer, F.: How does investor sentiment affect stock market crises? Evidence from panel data. Recherche 46, 723–747 (2010)

Biographies

Stewart Jones' specialist area in research is corporate financial reporting. Stewart's research interests cover such topics as credit risk and corporate distress analysis, accounting theory, standard setting, international standards harmonization, financial analysis and research methodology (with a particular interest in discrete choice modelling and stated preference experiments). Stewart's industry experience includes the interpretation of accounting standards; financial analysis and regulation; credit risk modelling and corporate performance analysis.

Maurice Peat has a PhD in Finance from UTS, in the area of theoretical and empirical financial distress modelling. Maurice has broad experience in business related disciplines, having worked in Economics and Information Systems. Maurice's current research interests cover such topics as credit risk and corporate distress analysis, a managerial decision context for financial analysis, the economics of restructuring transactions and the impacts of Information technology on financial innovation.

© Springer International Publishing Switzerland 2015
A. Lugmayr (Ed.): FinanceCom 2014, LNBIP 217, pp. 135–138, 2015.
DOI: 10.1007/978-3-319-28151-3

Stefan Feuerriegel is a PhD student at Chair of Information Systems Research of the University of Freiburg with a focus on text mining and sentiment analysis of financial news. He holds a Master of Science in Simulation Sciences from the RWTH Aachen University. He has co-authored research publications in the European Journal of Operational Research, Optimization Engineering and the Journal of Decision Systems.

Dirk Neumann is Full Professor with the Chair of Information Systems of the University of Freiburg, Germany. His research topics include Business Analytics, Text Mining and Cloud Computing. He studied information systems in Giessen (Diploma), Economics in Milwaukee, WI, USA (Master) and received a PhD from Karlsruhe Institute of Technology (KIT) in 2004. He has (co-)authored many research publications at European Journal of Operational Research, ACM Transactions on Internet Technology, Journal of Management of Management Information Systems or Decision Support Systems.

Islam Qudah is a PhD student at the School of Computer Science and Engineering at the University of New South Wales (UNSW) in Australia. Islam's research interest is in the field of news sentiment analysis and financial markets data analysis. Islam holds an honours degree in Computer Science from University of Technology Sydney (2010), and a master's degree in Information Technology from University of Western Sydney (2003). Islam has an extensive industry experience in the field of data processing/data analyses and has worked for many organisations in Australia and abroad.

Fethi A. Rabhi is a Professor in the School of Computer Science and Engineering at the University of New South Wales (UNSW) in Australia. He is currently actively involved in several research projects in the area of large-scale news and financial market data analysis. He completed a PhD in Computer Science at the University of Sheffield in 1990 and held several academic appointments in the USA and the UK before joining UNSW in 2000.

Antal Ratku is working on his Master's Thesis at Chair of Information Systems Research of the University of Freiburg with a focus on text mining and sentiment analysis of financial news. He holds a Bachelor's degree in economics from the Corvinus University of Budapest.

Weisi Chen is a final year PhD candidate in the School of Computer Science and Engineering at the University of New South Wales (UNSW) in Australia. His research focus is leveraging different technologies to support financial market data analysis for researchers. Taking advantage of his research work, he is currently also working as a casual eResearch trainer in Intersect Australia.

Martin Haferkorn is a research assistant at the Chair of Business Administration, especially e-Finance at Goethe-University Frankfurt and a research associate of the E-Finance Lab, an industry-academic partnership between Frankfurt and Darmstadt Universities and major players within the financial industry. His research focuses on business information systems and finance, in particularly in the areas of algorithmic trading, regulation and crypto-currencies. His work has been presented at major conferences such as EFA, ICIS and ECIS.

Michael Siering is a postdoctoral researcher at Goethe University Frankfurt and a research associate at the E-Finance Lab, an industry-academic partnership between Goethe University Frankfurt and several industry partners. He has been a visiting scholar at Penn State University. His research focuses on decision support systems in electronic markets, with a focus on the analysis of user generated content by means of sentiment analysis and text mining. His work has been published in Decision Support Systems and major conference proceedings such as ICIS, ECIS and HICSS. He holds a Ph.D. in business administration from Goethe University Frankfurt.

Kai Zimmermann is a research assistant at the Chair of Business Administration, especially e-Finance at Goethe-University Frankfurt and a research associate of the E-Finance Lab, an industry-academic partnership between Frankfurt and Darmstadt Universities and major players within the financial industry. His scientific work focuses on regulation in securities trading as well as empirical market microstructure and is regularly presented at international conferences and meetings.

Alberto Palazzesi is Graduated in business administration at the Catholic University of the Sacred Heart, Alberto is Ph.D candidate in Financial Markets and Institutions. His academic research activities deal with Big Data, technology implementation and ambidexterity. Since 2011 he joined CeTIF - Center of Research in Banking & Finance Innovation and Organization where he performs researches on the banking and insurance industries.

Chiara Frigerio got a Ph.D in Informations Systems and Organizations Studies.

She is assistant professor of Organization Science and Decision Support Systems at Cattolica University of Sacred Heart, in Milan.

From 2001, she is research manager at CeTIF - Center of Research in Banking & Finance Innovation and Organization belonging to the same university. She coordinates EU as well as national research projects about innovation practices in the financial industry. She is author of several papers and books on the process and IT innovation.

Federico Rajola holds a degree in Banking and Finance as well as a PhD in Information Systems Management.

He is professor at the Management Faculty of the Catholic University of Milan where he teaches Project Management and Organization Studies and visiting at INSEAD. He is scientific director of CeTIF a research Centre on Technology, Innovation and Finance of the Catholic University.

He has chaired several International academic conferences and workshops. He has authored several papers and books on Information Systems, Business Intelligence, CRM and Innovation in Organizations.

He has co-ordinated and managed several Innovative European research projects under the programme Esprit and IST.

Josué Manuel Quintana Diaz is a Ph.D. scholarship holder of the Heinrich-Böll-Foundation, investigating with his thesis in the field of institutional economics, which forms part of the cluster on 'Transformation Research'. As associated member of the excellence cluster 'The Formation of Normative Orders', the DFG Graduate School 'Value and Equivalence' and the Goethe GRADE "Center Sustain". Besides his research concentration he engages in collaborative projects related to the "blockchain technology" as way to promote Decentralized Autonomous Organizations (DAO), bringing together expertise in the field of institutions, management of complex systems and sustainable organizational behavior. Before starting his Ph.D. Josué Quintana Diaz worked at KfW Development Bank as Project Manager in charge for international development finance programs focused on renewable energy project finance and climate change initiatives on behalf of the Federal Ministry of Development and Economic Cooperation (BMZ).

Artur Lugmayr is Associate Professor at Curtin University, Australia, where he teaches and supervises students in visualization technologies, interactive media, media management, and digital humanities. Artur was Professor for digital media management at the Tampere University of Technology (TUT), Finland 2009–2014 establishing the Entertainment and Media Management Laboratory and the New Ambient Multimedia Laboratory 2004–2009. Artur holds a Dr.-Techn. degree (Information Technology, TUT), and is pursuing his Dr.-Arts studies at Aalto University, Helsinki, Finland in motion pictures. He was visiting scientist in Singapore, Brisbane, Austria, Ghana; since 2000 1.5+ MEUR funding; 170+ publications; 24+ invited keynotes; and 27+ invited guest lectures. http://www.artur-lugmayr.com

Author Index

Printed in the United States
By Bookmasters